SEEKING WHOLENESS

SEEKING WHOLENESS

Women Dealing with *Abuse of Power* in the Catholic Church

~

MARIE EVANS BOUCLIN

LITURGICAL PRESS
Collegeville, Minnesota

www.litpress.org

Cover design by Joachim Rhoades, O.S.B.

Parts of this book originally appeared in Pour vivre debout: femmes et pouvoir dans l'Église (Montréal: Mediaspaul, 2000). They are used and translated here with the permission of the publisher.

The Scripture quotations contained herein are from the New Revised Standard Version Bible: Catholic Edition, © 1989, 1993, Division of Christian Education of the National Council of the Churches of Christ in the United States of America. Used by permission. All rights reserved.

| 1 | 2 | 3 | 4 | 5 | 6 | 7 | 8 |

Library of Congress Cataloging-in-Publication Data

Bouclin, Marie Evans.
    Seeking wholeness : women dealing with abuse of power in the Catholic Church / Marie Evans Bouclin.
        p.   cm.
    "Parts of this book originally appeared in Pour vivre debout: femmes et pouvoir dans l'église"—T.p. verso.
    Summary: "Helps women and men, victims and non-victims, to understand and act against sexual abuse and the abuse of power"— Provided by publisher.
    Includes bibliographical references and index.
    ISBN-13: 978-0-8146-2240-7 (pbk. : alk. paper)
    ISBN-10: 0-8146-2240-2 (pbk. : alk. paper)
    1. Women in the Catholic Church.   2. Catholic women—Abuse of. 3. Abused women—Religious life.   4. Catholic Church—Clergy— Psychology.   5. Catholic Church—Clergy—Sexual behavior.   I. Bouclin, Marie Evans. Pour vivre debout. English. Selections.   II. Title.

BX2347.8.W6B69   2006
282'.082—dc22

                                                                2005018518

CONTENTS

ACKNOWLEDGMENTS

This book is dedicated to the many women who shared with me their story of abuse at the hands of clergy and also to those women and men who are searching for ways to help them in their healing. I could not have written this book had I not had the privilege of studying theology at the Université de Sherbrooke, particularly with Louise Melançon who eventually directed my thesis on the subject of this book, and Marie Gratton who opened my mind to feminist theological reading and reflection. To my friends of the *Sourdough* community, especially Barbara Organ, Gertrud Jaron Lewis, and Susan de Gruchy, I owe a debt of thanks for their sound and generous advice. My friend and colleague Deborah Jongsma deserves a great deal of credit for revising the translation of parts of this book originally published in French, as does Lise Cousineau for her help in doing the research. I also wish to thank Dolores Hall for her invaluable hours of editing. Above all, I am grateful to my husband Albert and our children, Suzanne, Dan, Robert, and his wife Chantal, for their affection and constant support.

INTRODUCTION

This book actually began February 17, 1992. At the end of my workday, my bishop handed me a letter typed by my assistant and dictated by his lawyer in which he told me that newspaper reports of my participation at a workshop for women in the church had been "embarrassing to the image of the church" and had raised questions as to my "suitability of continued employment." The next morning, the bishop told me I could continue working, not as his personal secretary and translator to the diocesan synod, but doing some translation and filing in a back office. Strangely enough, the newspaper article had also sparked a rash of letters and calls thanking me for speaking out against the oppression of women in the church. When they learned I had been demoted because of the workshop, many women began telling me their stories of abuse of power at the hands of clergy. One of the calls that same day came from a woman I happened to know in a diocesan marriage tribunal, telling me in tears that she had just been summarily fired.

After a few weeks of working in this very stressful environment, my doctor suggested I resign. I had all the symptoms of burnout, he said, and no job was worth keeping at the price of my health. So I asked for a month's sick leave that extended into five months, after which I tendered my resignation. To his credit, the diocesan treasurer continued to pay my salary during this time. This gave me the time I needed to rebuild my health. I thank him here for his kindness and compassion. Today I can also thank my bishop. Working for the diocesan corporation gave me a much clearer understanding of the patriarchal and power-centered dynamics at work within the institutional church, but having to leave that setting gave me the freedom I needed to work with and on behalf of women who had been hurt by the church. In fact it gave me back my life.

As I listened to the many disturbing stories of women who had been dismissed from church work, from a pastoral assistant who was fired by a new pastor to a seminary professor who had been dismissed for signing a petition advocating the ordination of women, I realized how truly fortunate I had been. I returned to my freelance translation business that afforded me the means and the opportunity to continue my studies in theology. This in turn exposed me to a whole new way of understanding both my Christian faith and the Catholic Church.

Then, in September of 1996, a friend of mine called in tears to tell me she had just ended a three-year "affair" with her pastor because he was sexually involved with another woman. She came to me for help because she felt I might understand her anger and frustration. In shock, I had no idea what to do. This book recounts my own journey of searching for ways to help.

More recently, we've been very focused on cases of sexual abuse of children by priests. The Catholic clergy (and their sexual mores) is increasingly put under the microscope of public scrutiny and called to accountability because the abuse of children, be it sexual, physical, or emotional, runs counter to our most basic ethical instincts and Christian beliefs. The Gospel is absolutely clear: Jesus, in the Gospel of Matthew (18:6), says that if we harm or scandalize children, it would be better for us to "have a great millstone fastened to our neck and be thrown into the depth of the sea." It is all the more intolerable in a Christian context because the Gospel commands us to protect our children from harm and scandal. We are rightly indignant and scandalized by the sexual abuse and exploitation of children, and try to find its causes in the celibacy requirement for priests. Their lack of emotional support and inadequate training in dealing with their own sexuality in the seminary are certainly contributing factors to the problem, but in society, we acknowledge that sexual abuse is not primarily about sex but about power.

Unfortunately, when it comes to dealing with the sexual abuse or exploitation of adult women (or men), there seems to be an underlying assumption that these people were "consenting adults," willingly engaged in a sexual or otherwise unhealthy relationship with their pastor or spiritual advisor. And so these abuses are not taken seriously because true consent is misunderstood. As Dominican canon lawyer Thomas Doyle observed when the U.S. Bishops' National Review Board Report and The John Jay Report were made public,

> The revelations of widespread sexual abuse of children and young people has surfaced concern for another aspect of clergy sexual abuse that is deep seated, equally insidious yet somewhat protected by a less than sensitive society. . . . There is far more sexual abuse of age appropriate victims, most of whom are women.[1]

Here again, the real issue is power. Even with the increasing presence of women in all spheres of social and professional activities, and the access of women to studies in theology, more and more devout Catholic women have had to face the gaping discrepancy between the Christian teaching about equality between men and women and the actual practice of equality within our communities. In the Catholic Church, all the decision-making power rests in the hands of men invested with the "sacred power" of the ordained priesthood, in a descending order from the pope and the Roman Curia to bishops or heads of men's religious orders to priests. The laity, which includes all women, have only a consultative voice in any decision that affects either the universal church or the local parish. When sacred power is misused or abused, the confidence of the faithful in their church leadership is undermined, and those who are victimized become emotionally, spiritually, and often physically ill. These tragic consequences have yet to be acknowledged in any official way, other than to call ordained men to a more virtuous life. Some attempts have been made by national bishops' conferences to deal with the problem of sexual abuse of children. And because there have been criminal charges brought against priests and bishops, many dioceses, particularly in North America, have developed policies to deal with allegations of sexual misconduct.

When these allegations involve women, however, the subject is still largely taboo. If it is raised at all, it is usually because some formal complaint has been made or a woman has gone before the civil courts and obtained an undisclosed, but presumably large, monetary settlement. Most cases are cloaked in secrecy, rumor, and innuendo to the point that the truth surrounding the events is seldom brought to light and the causes, circumstances, and perverse effects of clergy abuse of power are never dealt with. The victims most grievously hurt are women who become involved in a sexual relationship with a priest who is their spiritual advisor or pastor. According to Reverend Marie Fortune, the founding director of the Centre for Prevention of Family and Sexual Violence, who counsels victims of sexual abuse in the pastoral relationship, sexual intercourse between a priest and a parishioner seeking pastoral help constitutes both sexual abuse and professional misconduct, because the power differential between them is too great.

A second group of women abused by clergy are those who dedicate their whole lives to their work for the church only to be summarily dismissed at the whim of the priest or bishop who employs them or when there is a change of parish or diocesan administration. Theologian Anne Carr points out that women are actively engaged in all aspects of church ministry for which "they are often overworked and not adequately paid" but they are "barred from full recognition and sacramental completion of the service they are already fulfilling."[2]

Official pronouncement on the power dynamic at work between women and ordained men in the Catholic Church[3] has not proved very helpful in addressing the problem that arises when members of Catholic communities are made aware of such abuses. Given the Gospel imperative to reach out to the hungry, the sick, the homeless, and the broken-hearted, how do we help heal the wounds of those who have suffered sexual abuse or exploitation at the hands of ordained men? How do we help them maintain their Christian faith and their sense of belonging to the church when the ministers of that faith, the leaders of that church, have betrayed their trust?

This was the challenge we faced when the director of a sexual assault clinic and I attempted to set up a support group for women who had been sexually abused by clergy. We found the task extremely difficult. When we asked the women, all practicing Catholics, if they wanted to get together to share their experiences and help each other "get back on their feet" and achieve some measure of physical, emotional, and spiritual wholeness, none wanted to get involved. For reasons that escaped us, these women didn't want to tell their stories or hear anyone else's. They felt both ashamed and responsible for what had happened to them. They also seemed to be afraid that expressing any anger or resentment over the misconduct of a member of the clergy could bring harm to the whole church. How could these women find emotional and spiritual healing if they couldn't even consider the possibility that it was not they but the priest who had acted inappropriately? Our first task was to convince them that tackling a problem in the church is not the same thing as denying one's faith, a distinction that was not clear to them.

Similarly, women who had been employed by the church and dismissed for no clear reason seemed unable to acknowledge that they had been victims of injustice. Having devoted enormous amounts of time and energy to their work in a parish or diocesan setting, and having made huge sacrifices for their faith and the mission of the church, they had been summarily cast aside because there was a change of pastor or because they had burnt out on the job, yet they expressed no interest in setting up a support group to help themselves and others. For them, as well, any criticism of clergy behavior was tantamount to disloyalty to God and the church.

I shared these concerns with a vowed religious who worked as a counselor and spiritual advisor to women alcoholics or women living with an alcoholic or a drug addict. She ventured the opinion that the women's strong reluctance to seek help outside the institutional church could be attributed to a kind of dependency in women upon the clergy that prevented them from questioning the way women are treated in the church. We were both familiar with the works of Anne Wilson Schaef, a psychotherapist who deals extensively with the psychological and social dynamics of addictions, codependence, and the systems that support them. Those readings made us suspect that the dependency of women in the church regarding clergy was actually a codependence problem. So, while the codependence theory will have its detractors, I include a description of codependent behaviors, based on the better-known publications on the subject, because I recognized so many of its traits in the women I interviewed.

Since those first attempts at starting a support group for women abused by clergy, many more women have crossed my path and have shared their painful stories. One of the most poignant was a woman who asked if she could come to our group even though she subsequently married the priest who raped and impregnated her. She was not the first, nor the last, woman who married a priest to come for help. There were also women who stayed in abusive marriages because their pastor had insisted it was their duty to honor their Catholic marriage vows by enduring the abuse heaped on them by a violent spouse. How, I wondered, could we minister to their needs?

We can begin by listening to the painful stories. We can learn from the women themselves how some have rebuilt their lives and found healing and wholeness. Hopefully this little book does this and also provides some insight to those called to journey with women who have very nearly been destroyed by an abuse of power by clergy.

Personal testimonies are the key element of the following pages. Out of respect for the sacredness of their stories and at their request, their real names are not given, and all identifying details have been omitted, but their stories are true and the issues they raise are very real. My hope is that the women in the church who are living in a situation of clergy abuse will find compassion and understanding here, some helpful suggestions for dealing with their pain, and ultimately, pathways to the peace and joy of a renewed faith.

Notes

1. Thomas P. Doyle, *The John Jay Report and The National Review Board Report* (www.justgoodcompany.com, 2004, 6).

2. Anne E. Carr, *Transforming Grace* (New York: Continuum, 1996) 39.

3. This issue was the subject of a Vatican document entitled "Letter to the Bishops of the Catholic Church on the Collaboration of Men and Women in the Church and in the World" (Congregation for the Doctrine of the Faith, May 31, 2004).

Chapter 1

UNCOVERING THE PROBLEM

Women who have been sexually abused by a priest or lost their employment in the church will not be helped by suggestions that they are hypersensitive, unbalanced, or even clergy-dependent, and therefore should simply find a good therapist or join the appropriate support group, should such a group exist where they live. While both suggestions would prove helpful, neither addresses the real issue: the women have been betrayed by their church. Before abused women can even consider that possibility, their stories must be heard and believed, and their very real pain and loss acknowledged. Recounting their experience helps them and those called to help them discover several commonalities, and allows us to label the oppression that afflicts them, namely, that they are victims of sexual abuse or exploitation. Once we've named the affliction, we can begin to look for ways to help, following Christ's example in Luke 13:11-13, lending a hand that will hopefully "enable her to stand up straight, set free from her ailment."

JOCELYN'S STORY

Jocelyn, an attractive-looking nurse in her late thirties, was married to a physician and was the mother of two teenagers. For some time, she had suspected her husband was having an affair. Eventually, he admitted the truth, asked for a divorce, and left. Since then, she had been confiding in Father Michael, a warm, understanding, and kind man in his late forties. The day that her divorce became final, Michael encouraged her to apply for an annulment, assuring her that he would help her fill out the

1

complicated forms. As she left his office that day, he hugged her a little more affectionately than usual, kissed her on the mouth, and said, "I really love you, you know." Jocelyn was confused and very uncomfortable. She hadn't heard those words or felt the comfort of a good hug in a long time. Michael suggested that Jocelyn could come to the rectory to fill out her annulment forms, preferably in the evening when things were quieter. The first time she went, and despite her reluctance, she went to bed with him. Michael asked her not to tell anyone. Jocelyn felt ashamed and guilty because Michael was her pastor and spiritual advisor, the person in whom she had confided her deepest secrets, and he did seem to offer her the love that was missing in her life.

Jocelyn began to notice that she often had to lie to her children and her friends about what was going on between her and Michael, and also about why she had no inclination to pick up the pieces of her life or date other men. Her children stopped attending Mass and openly showed their dislike of Michael. They seemed to be aware of what was going on between them, became increasingly resentful toward Jocelyn, and once hinted that her closeness to Michael might have driven her husband to adultery.

Two years after her divorce, Jocelyn received her marriage annulment. She asked Michael to leave the priesthood and marry her. His answer was, "I want to be a priest and the church does not allow priests to marry. Take it or leave it." Jocelyn was so distraught that she consulted a therapist. When she told him her story, he could barely contain his anger: "If I slept with one of my clients, I'd be sued for professional misconduct. So would your doctor, or any other professional. Drop that man and report him to his bishop." But Jocelyn was afraid to report Michael to his bishop because it would mean the end of their relationship. Late one evening several months later, she dropped in unexpectedly on Michael and found him with another woman. She began to wonder if he hadn't just been using her all along.

Jocelyn's children have now grown up and left home. She has few women friends, can find only part-time work, and is barely getting by. She is under psychiatric care because she is continually battling depression and has attempted suicide.

NANCY'S STORY

Nancy and Jack had been married for about ten years. Jack owned a car dealership. Business was very good, and he was happy that Nancy could stay at home with their four children. He supported Nancy in her desire to do community work and occasionally helped her with the parish youth group and at the local soup kitchen. One day their pastor, Father Francis, who was elderly and had cancer, asked Nancy to help him with the sacramental preparation of the younger children of the parish. He was expecting the bishop to appoint an assistant any day. What the large, inner-city parish really needed was a pastoral assistant, someone who not only had some theological training and could communicate well with the younger families, but who also had the means to work largely as a volunteer. Nancy, who had thought about becoming a nun when she was a young woman, believed the Spirit was now calling her to serve the church in a more official capacity.

A few months later Mark, the new assistant, arrived. He could see what an asset Nancy was to the life of the parish. People respected her and trusted her judgment. She loved her work and wanted to make a career of it, so she had registered for the ministries training program offered by her diocese. Mark complimented her on her fine work, encouraged her to keep up her studies in theology, and confided with her about his struggle with alcoholism, the loneliness of the celibate life, and his own plans to go back to school so he could apply for a teaching position at a university. He asked her for advice on any number of pastoral problems and delegated many of his own tasks to her. She often prepared his homilies so he could study, and filled in for him at some parish committee meetings. She realized that Mark did not want to be a parish priest all his life, that he aspired to "greater things."

Nancy's husband would occasionally complain that she spent too much time at the parish and that her salary was ridiculous considering her qualifications, workload, and level of responsibility. He was annoyed that she talked about Mark so much. Her children complained about her lack of interest in their achievements. One day her seventeen-year-old daughter became totally frustrated with her and told her to face the fact that she was in love with Mark and should get a divorce. Nancy was flabbergasted. She admitted that she really enjoyed working with Mark, but was convinced that their friendship was based on their mutual love for God and the church. They made a great team, but there was definitely nothing "sexual" going on. What made her happy, she felt, was that she shared in Mark's priestly ministry. Her husband, on the other hand, had become a workaholic and drank a lot. The children could hardly wait to leave home.

After several years, Father Francis died and Father Mark accepted a teaching position at a seminary. The new pastor felt that Nancy had far too much influence in the parish and, in any case, he had no real need for a pastoral assistant. When a woman in the parish hinted that Nancy and Mark "had been an item," the new pastor summarily dismissed her. Nancy was left without a job, in a floundering marriage, and severely depressed.

THE CHURCH'S FORGOTTEN WOMEN

The stories of Jocelyn and Nancy are composites based on the stories of eighteen different women. Except for two structured interviews, I heard their stories over coffee, after a meeting or workshop on women in the church, and once from a woman who was seeking help for a friend and found in the process that she herself had been abused. When I was asked to assist with a self-help group, I took notes on the conversations under fictitious names and filled in one of two questionnaires (reproduced at the end of this book) that had been drawn up with the help of the addiction counselor mentioned earlier. She had heard similar stories, and felt there was a need for a support group for women who had been victims of clergy misconduct. We adapted the questionnaire used with new members of *Adult Children of Alcoholics*, a twelve-step program for people who have grown up in a dysfunctional family. In searching for commonalities in the various stories and in the answers to the questionnaires, I remembered other incidents I was told about when I worked in the diocesan office. I tried to contact the women who had told me about their problems, but none of them wanted to "reopen old wounds." They felt they had to protect their families and did not want to jeopardize their jobs with the parish or the diocese.

From all the stories, a picture emerged of two distinct groups of women who had been deeply hurt: those who had been in an abusive sexual relationship, and those who had been dismissed, with no reason given, from a parish or diocesan position. Both situations involved the abuse of power, in different forms. None of the respondents seemed to want to lay any blame on the priest who had hurt her or on a religious system that tolerated such abuses. This willingness to protect the abusive priest made me even more suspicious that these women might be in a state of codependence with clergy, much like women who live with an alcoholic, a drug addict, or a battering partner.

None of the women would have called themselves codependent, although they acknowledged that they were very hurt by the way they had been treated by the clergy. They admitted to struggling with fatigue and many other physical ailments, that they were often depressed, or even suicidal. Devout, practicing Catholics at the outset, most of the women said they had left the church because they could no longer live out their Christian faith in a church that was so blatantly male and power-centered; three of them said they had lost their faith altogether. Only two women admitted to being clergy-dependent, or, as one put it, a "churchaholic in recovery."

Helping us reach out to these women were three counselors, experienced in working with abused women. One is a nun who was in charge of the training and spiritual counseling of younger members of her community. Her input was all the more valuable in that some of the women abused by clergy are or have been members of a religious order. The second woman was an Anglican priest who was often called upon to help victims of incest and family violence. The third was a therapist working with survivors of incest and child sexual abuse. Their collective wisdom is reflected in the suggested avenues of spiritual healing that will be discussed further on.

As I mentioned, the details of the stories related at the beginning of this chapter are not those of two specific women. In that sense they are fictitious, but the problem of abuse of power in the church is no less real, and the stories tell nothing that was not experienced by several women. As a matter of fact, every woman I interviewed told me that she knew of at least one other woman who had been treated as she had; one of them knew of six other women emotionally and physically abused by the same priest.

Jocelyn's story is meant to illustrate that women who become involved in a sexual relationship with a priest are victims of sexual assault. Assault is not too strong a word, as what follows will show that we are not dealing with consensual sexual activity. Women like Nancy, on the other hand, who are devastated by the loss of their church employment, are victims of systematic discrimination and sexual exploitation. The codependence that develops in all these women is directly related to an abuse of the clergy's power, a practice which is a negation of Christian values. A woman who has experienced abuse of power and who is trying to free herself from the hold that the priest has on her is very much like a battered spouse. She is still "in love" with the church that has rejected her or the priest who assaulted her. The woman feels responsible and guilty, yet she is sometimes unable to identify exactly what she did wrong. She refuses to question either the priest's behavior or the church that condoned it. Initially, she is prepared to forgive everything. In fact, she feels obligated to forgive, forget, and keep her pain a secret, because she is afraid—afraid of losing the support, friendship, or consideration of the priest, afraid of being ostracized by her parish community, afraid of being labeled a whore or a trouble-maker, afraid that if she makes a complaint she will bring into question the holiness of the church in the person of its priest. And it is precisely her fear of finding herself abandoned and alone, her sense of total helplessness vis-à-vis the priest and the church, that are the symptoms of a dependence upon clergy. As we will see, the dynamics of dependence and codependence are substantially the same.

Readings

The dynamic of clergy sexual abuse is best explained in the work of Reverend Dr. Marie Marshall Fortune: *Is Nothing Sacred?* (Cleveland: United Church Press, 1999); *Sexual Violence, The Unmentionable Sin* (New York: Pilgrim Press, 1983).

For a vowed religious woman's powerful testimony of sexual abuse, see Yvonne Maes, *The Cannibal's Wife: A Memoir* (New York: Herodias, Inc., 1999).

For the difficulties experienced by women working in the Catholic Church, read Anne E. Carr, *Transforming Grace* (New York: Continuum, 1996).

Chapter 2

NAMING THE PROBLEM

The term "codependence" surfaced in the 1970s to describe some family members of alcoholics. Its meaning was subsequently extended to apply to people who had grown up in an abusive or dysfunctional family, that is, one that fails to provide for the psychological and emotional needs of its members. Among these are families where there are alcohol, drug, or gambling addictions, incest, emotional, physical, or psychological violence, and strict religious fundamentalism. Children who grow up in such an environment tend to have very particular personality traits in adulthood. They have unhealthy ways of relating to themselves and to others. Their personal validation and sense of human dignity must come from outside of themselves. In other words, they look for approval and acceptance from others, be it a person, a group, or an institution. Codependent persons usually lack self-esteem, are unable to set personal boundaries, have difficulty knowing and expressing their own opinions and convictions, are frequently unable to meet their own needs and wants, and tend to be obsessive and given to excesses.

Anne Wilson Schaef, an American psychotherapist, has written extensively on codependence. She set out to explain it by analyzing the psychological, social, and political realities of women's lives in today's society. In describing what it is like for women to belong to a world in which white males have all the power, she speaks of the "original sin of being born female" in a patriarchal system that regards itself as sacred and is maintained by the following four myths: (1) it is the only system that exists; (2) men are intrinsically superior to women; (3) men know and understand everything, and therefore have the right to decide what is true and worth learning about; and (4) it is possible to be completely logical, rational, and objective within this system (disregarding all other ways of thinking, learning, and understanding).[1] In fact, these four myths can be summarized in one: the white male can be regarded as infallible God, at least as defined by the system.

This system confers on itself the right not only to define who women are and tell them how to think, feel, and act so that they consciously and unconsciously support the male patriarchal system and its myths; it also teaches women that they are fundamentally inferior by birth. Schaef even goes on to say that there is no "absolution" for the "sin" of being born female except through some external mediator who is always male. This system makes women believe that if they can succeed in finding a man and earning his approval and validation, they may obtain "absolution." This would explain why women go to such great lengths to please men and try to meet the requirements of the male patriarchal system, and why, in so doing, they find themselves in a state of total dependency on men.

Anne Wilson Schaef's analysis of women's reality is important for two reasons. She explains why women need to define their own reality so they can free themselves from a patriarchal system that oppresses them, and she stresses the importance of women becoming aware of the theological underpinnings of the patriarchal system. Schaef points out that the phenomenon of codependence has sprung up within this system, and goes on to describe it in more detail as a truly deadly disease:

> What we are calling codependence is, indeed, a disease that has many forms and expressions and that grows out of a disease process that is inherent in the system in which we live. I call this disease process the addictive process . . . an unhealthy and abnormal disease process, whose assumptions, beliefs, behaviors, and lack of spirituality lead to a process of nonliving that is progressively death-oriented.[2]

Her objective is to share her experience as a psychotherapist with women who want to be free of their codependence. In doing so, she provides us with signs to watch for as we listen to the testimonies of women who share their experiences of abuse of power in a patriarchal church.

Most of the women I met with did not like to use the word "codependent," even if they could find no other name for the way they felt. This is consistent with an increasingly common feminist critique of the term. Two major objections have surfaced. First, there is an objection to the prefix "co-" which could imply some type of collusion or reciprocal interaction, suggesting that women consent to their oppression and abuse. A second objection sees in the use of the term an implicit sexism that blames women for their own victimization. Does the term codependent mean that women who have been victims of the abuse of power have no one but themselves to blame for a problem that has much broader psychological, political, and social implications? The reality is that codependence, of course, is not found only in women. Anne Wilson Schaef, in her analysis of the phenomenon, states categorically that codependence is a societal disorder, largely because we live in a society where self-centeredness, dishonesty, and the illusion of control are the norm.[3]

Codependence is an outgrowth of a patriarchal society where the power structure is based on the domination of some men over other men and all women. Such a structure of domination justifies the victimizing of those dominated, men and women. And while both A. W. Schaef and feminist critics of codependence agree that codependent persons are obsessed with the desire to control the behavior of other people, especially those who are dominating them, it must be understood that they only demonstrate this desire with the goal of putting an end to the abuse of power of which they are victims.

Critics are quite right on one very important point. Codependence is a word that can be applied to women who are perfectly assimilated into a society dominated by men, and it describes precisely the manner in which women are trained to support such a system of domination and subordination. For women in the church, as in society at large, this training begins at birth and continues all through their lives, first in the family and then within certain institutions, particularly the church. The type of codependence found in Catholic women can be directly attributed to the fact that the Catholic Church, patriarchal institution par excellence, trains its clergy to take on a role of domination by entrusting to them alone, by way of priestly ordination, all the decision-making power. And while men in the church may be codependent, we must not let that fact obscure the real power dynamic of the church that maintains the existing inequality of men and women in a fundamentally sexist institution.

Without a doubt, the use of the term "codependence" is problematic. Actually, as we shall see in the following pages, the women we are dealing with are perhaps more akin to "battered women." As Joanne Carlson Brown and Rebecca Parker write, "The women who stay (in the church) are surely as victimized and abused as any battered woman."[4] Should we be talking about women's "victimization," their "extreme vulnerability," or simply the "oppression" of women in the church? Even if all of the above apply, *codependence*, in my experience, seems to be the phenomenon that best describes the state of a very large number of women in the Catholic Church today. Of course, it is impossible to discuss codependence without also mentioning the phenomenon of dependency. The dependency referred to here is the addiction members of the clergy have to power that closely resembles an addiction to alcohol or drugs. That, however, is not our focus here. It is the experience of a group of women that will help us understand to what degree victims of abuse of power by a clergy member exhibit signs of a codependence that is both caused and maintained by the institution. Here are some of the signs of codependence found in women who have been abused by clergy.

LACK OF GROUNDING FROM WITHIN

Codependent persons have no center or grounding from within, meaning that their understanding of who they are is determined from the outside, by others, so they have no ownership or real knowledge of their deepest selves. They have isolated themselves from their own feelings and emotions in order to better respond to those of others. They spend a great deal of time trying to guess what others want so they can please them. They live outside themselves and seek to fill their own inner needs and find happiness by meeting the needs of others. They spend all their physical and psychic energy meeting the wants and needs of another person, an institution, or their work. In a word, they have no idea who they really are. They are not aware of having an inner core, that place where they are completely, totally themselves. This lack of self-awareness and compulsion to please others is at the root of all other manifestations of codependence.

The codependent church woman has been cut off from her spiritual self. Her nature, her mission, her entire life has been defined by the teachings of the church. When we consider that no woman has ever had a voice in the formulation of any of this teaching, we realize that the Catholic woman's existence is determined largely by a system of beliefs, rituals, moral code, and spirituality devised historically by men whom she has been taught to trust. Her deepest self, her center, that place where she should be able to enter into and maintain a personal relationship with the divine, to experience the sacred, is only accessible through the mediation of the church's minister and sacraments. This lack of grounding in the self often takes the form of an extreme "neediness" characterized by a belief that they cannot find happiness or meaning in life unless there is someone (usually a man) totally dedicated to meeting their every emotional or spiritual need and lavishing attention on them.

When women like Jocelyn are asked why they did not simply say no to the priest who insisted on having a sexual relationship, they usually answer that they found they couldn't because they trusted the priest as a man of God; they believed that a priest is the closest thing to God; saying no to a priest would be tantamount to saying no to God. They have been taught to obey the priest, not their own inner voice or conscience. For the same reasons, women like Nancy would have done anything, including sacrificing all their personal needs and desires, to prove they were worthy servants of the church and deserving of clergy approval because earning clergy approval was the only way they could get God's approval. Their centers or core selves were not so much given over to God living within them as they were focused on meeting the requirements of the church as interpreted by its priest.

DENIAL

Codependent persons live in a state of denial, that is, they have convinced themselves and try to convince others and indeed the whole world that there is no problem. In fact, they cannot admit to themselves that they have a problem. Sexually abused women do not see their involvement with the priest as problematic; exploited women attribute only good intentions to the priest who fired them; they believe they are the cause of the problem. One of the most difficult things for these women to accept about the church is the fact that they are oppressed *because they are women*, that someone has used their desire to serve God and the church for their own selfish purposes, or that the institution has kept itself in power by taking advantage of their availability and generosity. They are excessively selfless and giving of themselves, and unfortunately, they end up being broken or burned out.

LACK OF SELF-ESTEEM

Every human being needs to believe in her or his self-worth. Sometimes that worth is based on one's identity, which involves belonging to a family, a group, or an institution. The importance of the group gives value to each of its members, who in turn base their self-worth on their degree of loyalty to the group and its ideology. The Christian understanding of self-esteem, based on the conviction of being infinitely loved by God, who created all men and women equal and in the divine image, seems to elude them.

Women in the church who have lost or never had a true sense of their human dignity cannot esteem themselves of any value greater than that which the church grants them by way of approval and acceptance by members of its hierarchical clergy. This will usually depend on the priest closest to them, such as a pastor or spiritual director, or the priest or bishop who is their employer. Our society still measures a woman's worth by her social graces, moral integrity, dedication to work, and virtue. Many Catholic women remember and practice the axiom "Give till it hurts, and then give some more," but even then, they are not considered men's equals. Yet, the more they are asked to give, the more they do give, in a futile attempt to be recognized as equals. Many women reported doing work for which a priest or a bishop got all the credit. Nancy described all the work she did as a lay pastoral assistant responsible for preparing children to receive the sacraments, and then she would prepare Mark's homily. Why? "Because he said I was much closer to the real lives of the people in the parish, and besides, he said it would help me meditate on the next Sunday's readings. No one knew I wrote his homilies, but people often told him how meaningful they were. He would never have admitted they were my work." So why would she do this? "Because we are here to serve, not to be praised."

After she was dismissed, Nancy began to think about how she had been manipulated. Her remarks echoed those of many church workers and volunteers. They believed they were contributing to the mission of the church without ever considering the structures of power that benefited from their service. It would seem that the vast majority of women are oblivious to the power structure in the church because they have no access to the inner circle of authority where decisions are made. Clerical power is an abstract and theoretical notion, and since women usually live out their faith commitment on a day-to-day basis at a very practical level, they only become aware of power structures when there are rules imposed on them that limit their actions.

But until they realize how their actions are limited by the structures of power, women like Nancy often burn out. Often they have lost touch with what first motivated their service to the church, the result of an active prayer life and intimate relationship with God, and so they feel they need to be valued, appreciated, and acknowledged by others for their so-called good works. They *do* so much that they find it difficult to take time for themselves. In the seven years Nancy worked for the parish, she took only one week off, and that was because her husband had won a week's vacation in Acapulco for selling the most cars for his firm. Any other holiday time she had was spent taking theology courses and pursuing her training as a pastoral assistant. Her professional qualifications had become an obsession.

Jocelyn, on the other hand, was grateful at first for Michael's support. She felt inadequate, wondering if her husband had left her because she was not good enough for him. She came to realize, however, that her needs were of no real concern in her relationship with Michael. She tried very hard to please him so he would not leave her. Though she was not overweight, she had developed bulimia because Michael had made a passing remark about "chubby women." They always met when it was convenient for him; and he would have her come to the rectory for an hour, then send her home, she said, "when his needs were met." She had become an object to him. Her children said she never ventured an opinion without referring to Michael. She also admitted that, before leaving him, she had never dared "look inside to find the place where she would meet God." Her whole life evolved around pleasing Michael.

LACK OF PERSONAL BOUNDARIES

Codependent people do not seem to know where their personal space begins and another's ends. They have no such boundaries because they have been taken from them. Anne Wilson Schaef claims that

> the family, the school, the church actively train us not to form boundaries. They teach us to think what we are told to think, feel what we are told to feel, see what we are told to see. . . . In order to have personal boundaries, a person must start with an internal referent (knowing what one feels and thinks from the inside) and then relate with the world from that perspective.[5]

Boundaries begin with respecting our bodily integrity. All the women who spoke to me mention, sometimes only in passing, that they had suffered some kind of sexual abuse in their childhood or teens. Nancy was a victim of incest when she was five years old. The memory surfaced when she was undergoing therapy. Jocelyn remembered that a priest had asked her to masturbate him when she had gone for spiritual direction at the age of fourteen. She had put the incident out of her mind until our conversation. A counselor who worked with victims of sexual assault noted that among the many women who came to their center and had been abused by clergy, the vast majority had been child victims of incest. The priest, she said, being a man of God and considered trustworthy, can easily abuse the trust placed in him. Children who have been taught to trust and obey adults, especially parents and priests because they represent God, are especially prone to becoming their victims. Many have been taught that respecting authority means not questioning, even something they suspect may be wrong. In adulthood this can translate into an inability to say no to authority figures such as a priest. Calling the priest "Father" is only one indication of the parental role he plays in the spiritual lives of the faithful. Nancy describes how a priest first crossed her boundaries:

Father Mark had been in our parish only a few weeks. One day, he came and sat in my office and told me an off-color joke. I was very embarrassed and must have blushed, but did not dare tell him he was out of line. He would often comment on my clothes or my hair, or stand so close when talking to me that I had to back away. I now realize he deliberately embarrassed me to show me that he was in control. He had the power and could invade my personal space.

NEED TO PLEASE

Part of seeking to receive external validation is a compulsive need to please people. Codependents worry a great deal not only about other people's needs but even about their slightest whims and desires, because they feel that if they can satisfy them, they will gain approval and acceptance. Many pastoral assistants tell of writing their pastor's sermons and doing other work for him so he could devote more time to his priestly duties. Nancy tells of doing much of Mark's work so he could pursue his studies. She had already been dismissed when he finished his graduate degree. He sent her a note thanking her for her help on a post card. Why did she do all that unpaid work? "I felt that I was freeing him up to do more important things—his ministry. A lot of the time he was out on the golf course!" Imagine the anger in that comment. She would never have vented that anger when she worked with Mark. Trained to deny their own feelings, codependent women suppress their anger or deny that they are being manipulated, treated unfairly, undervalued, or ridiculed, because they are naive and excessively devoted. This is accompanied by a marked mistrust of one's own perceptions and a fear of paying attention to one's feelings. It is also a way of making oneself invisible. In constantly trying to please authority figures in the church, women lose themselves. Striving to please others is touted as a virtue in women, yet it is often perceived as a sign of weakness in men.

COMPULSION TO CONTROL

Pleasing, of course, is an oblique way of trying to control people and situations by making oneself indispensable. Having no center or self-concept, codependent people do for others what others could do for themselves. They are slaves to perceived duty, suffer without complaining, accept any and all blame and responsibility for the mistakes of others. That is why it is so easy to say that a woman who has a sexual relationship with a priest is a seductress. She herself feels she is to blame. Had she not been attractive, the priest would not have "succumbed." That is also why women in the church tend to burn out—they can never do enough or do it well enough to be considered equals. That equality is a right, not a reward, seems to escape them because their experience has taught them that in the church, equality between women and priests is an illusion.

Codependents also acquire the reputation of being controllers because they take life very seriously and feel that they have to find solutions for everybody's problems. They feel they are personally responsible for what others think, feel, and do, but because they have no real control, they become very manipulative. Their life is a paradox. Having no personal boundaries, they do not know where their self ends and the self of others begins, so they internalize everything. Women working for the church, who give of themselves so readily, usually feel they should know about everything. This is how they manipulate the people they work for, creating an inner illusion that they have control or a certain measure of power. Of course, some do, but it is only a power of influence, a very fleeting power which can be lost as soon as there is a change in church administration.

SELF-CENTEREDNESS

The need to do everything for everybody is actually part of being self-centered. How can people who have no center, no boundaries, and are never in touch with their own feelings believe they are indispensable? Because to them everything that happens to the priest, good or bad, is their fault; they feel personally responsible for the survival of the church. That is what motivated Nancy to do most of Mark's work—to free him up to fulfill his priestly duties. Jocelyn would not report Michael to his bishop because she was afraid he would be disciplined, and if the truth came out, it would cause a scandal and drive parishioners away from the church—and that would all be her fault!

LOSS OF INTEGRITY

Another characteristic of codependence is a loss of personal integrity. What is morally right or wrong is no longer clear, no longer based on personal conscience but on what the clergy tells them. Real motives for doing things become unclear for the codependent woman because others have set out criteria of behavior that are extremely self-serving, not for her but for them. She may well rationalize her choices and try to hide her desire for the approval and acceptance of others. She will usually avoid everything and everybody who would make her face up to the fact that she is living in an abusive relationship.

Women in the church have been trained to accept that what clergy tells them is right—even if their conscience tries to tell them differently. When a woman believes a priest who tells her that sexual activity is an acceptable element of pastoral care, or that dedication to the parish must take precedence over everything else, including her health, personal life, and spiritual development, she loses her moral grounding. It is very difficult for her to accept that she has been abused, lied to, manipulated, and violated in her very soul.

Facing this truth is frightening. There is always the risk of being rejected or abandoned, of failing or of disappointing others, and being punished for it. This fear creates a rigid attitude that can often be detected in their body language. A therapist who has worked for years with battered women and women living with an alcoholic or a drug addict says she often recognizes abused women by their demeanor. They are carefully groomed but tense and evasive about what is really going on in their own lives. They have little or no self-esteem; still, they can be very critical of others as of themselves. They are unhappy, disconnected from reality, and bitter, but they try to maintain a façade that belies the fact that they have neglected their physical, mental, emotional, and spiritual well-being. Their body language and critical attitude are attempts to mask the pain they feel inside.

HEALTH PROBLEMS

Women in the church who have suffered this kind of abuse at the hands of a priest adopt a form of behavior that is not conducive to a healthy body, mind, or spirit. Clergy codependents invariably end up in very poor health, which can be a blessing in disguise, because when they have to go and see a doctor or a therapist, there is a chance that the root cause of their ailment will be uncovered. Over the years that Jocelyn was Michael's "mistress," she had surgery for breast cancer, frequently had stomach flu, started smoking to curb her appetite, took large doses of tranquillizers, and began drinking fairly heavily. Nancy, a few months after Mark arrived in the parish, developed frequent back problems, stomach ulcers, and a hiatus hernia. Her doctor had once told her to quit her job because it had become too stressful. "Never," she replied, "I love my job too much. And besides, the parish needs me."

The poor state of health found in victims of abuse of power would appear to be the physical reflection of poor psychological and spiritual health, manifest in the ways they relate to themselves and to others. On the one hand, these women have internalized a structure of beliefs, behaviors, and spirituality that the clergy have used to their own advantage. Their complaints about these abuses have been too frequently either ignored, trivialized, ridiculed, or silenced. But as women begin to break the silence by sharing their experience and learning from one another, a healing process begins to emerge where women seek wholeness on their own terms. Healthier relationships between women and ordained men in the church will also emerge as women begin to see themselves, no longer as powerless victims of an oppressive religious system, but as full-fledged, adult members of an inclusive family of faith. This, as we shall see, hinges upon a better understanding of the priesthood as it exists in the Catholic Church today.

Readings

A very helpful book for Catholic women is Virginia Curran Hoffman, *The Codependent Church* (New York: Crossroad, 1991). A classic for understanding the relationship between traditional Christian teaching and violence against women is Joanne Carlson Brown and Carole R. Bohn, eds., *Christianity, Patriarchy and Abuse: A Feminist Critique* (New York: Pilgrim Press, 1989).

Notes

1. Anne Wilson Schaef, *Women's Reality: An Emerging Female System in a White Male Society* (Minneapolis: Winston, 1985) 8.

2. Anne Wilson Schaef, *Codependence Misunderstood—Mistreated* (HarperSanFrancisco, 1986) 25.

3. Anne Wilson Schaef, *When Society Becomes an Addict* (San Francisco: Harper and Row, 1987) 29–30.

4. J. Carlson Brown and C. R. Bohn, eds., *Christianity, Patriarchy and Abuse: A Feminist Critique* (New York: Pilgrim Press, 1989) 3.

5. Schaef, *Codependence Misunderstood—Mistreated*, 50.

Chapter 3

POWER AND THE PRIESTHOOD

There are many ways of looking at the priesthood as it exists in the Catholic Church. There is the official teaching of the church on the matter, and then there is the perception of Catholics in the pew. Sadly, in the case of ordinary Catholics, but more particularly women who have been abused by priests, one senses a naiveté, an almost infantile perception of religion, faith, the church, and its priesthood. This is in no way intended to lay blame on the victims. Like most Catholics, they learned about religion in the Catholic school system and never pursued the study of their faith beyond elementary school, except perhaps for brief instruction in preparation for marriage or the baptism of a child. Even among pastoral assistants and religious, faith education was carefully filtered through the exclusive lens of official Catholic teaching. Catholic laypeople were, by and large, discouraged from reading the Bible and from questioning anything that was preached from the pulpit. Criticism of a priest's behavior was certainly frowned upon when it was not harshly reprimanded or even punished. Indeed, until the sexual abuse of children scandal broke, most of us believed our priests to be God's representative among us, dedicated men of integrity who had a "corporate and personal call to be custodian and guardian of the identity of Jesus in the midst of the Church and the world."[1] Unfortunately, the pedophilia scandal was for many Catholics a loss of innocence, a time to face head on the reality that for all his sacred power to teach, govern and sanctify us, "Father" was not always modeling Jesus in our midst.

This is not meant to imply that all priests are sexual predators, nor that the women who were abused are any more naive or less intelligent than other Catholics. It simply means that the spiritual power of the church, which the hierarchy of the church reserves for itself, plays on a very clear separation between clergy and laity. This clergy–laity divide both denies and absolves the laity from true responsibility for their faith. Since the laity, which includes all women, even those with extensive training in theology, have had no part in developing official church doctrine, pastoral policy and liturgical practices, a significant proportion of Catholics remain in a state of spiritual infancy. The childish perception many Catholics have of the church and its leaders have made many of the faithful, especially devout and vulnerable women, particularly susceptible to being misled and abused by religious authorities. It is therefore crucial for women who wish to recover from an abuse of power to understand the *sacred power* conferred by holy orders at ordination.

CATHOLIC TEACHING ON THE PRIESTHOOD

A good place to start is with the *Catechism of the Catholic Church* (1993) written and promulgated as a result of the Second Vatican Council "[t]o guard and present better the precious deposit of Christian doctrine in order to make it more accessible to the Christian faithful and to all people of good will."[2] Article 1537 of the *Catechism* states that "the word *order* in Roman antiquity designated an established civil body, especially a governing body. . . ." This is a concept borrowed from the Roman Empire during the first centuries of Christianity when the church was developing a hierarchical structure and a legal framework based upon Roman law. The word *order* has come to designate the sacrament by which men are inducted into the order of bishops, priests or deacons, that is, those who are allowed to exercise "sacred power." Modeled on the sacrificial priesthood of the Old Testament, "a prefiguring of the ordained ministry of the New Covenant," the ministerial or hierarchical priesthood had as its primary purpose to bring about God's plan of salvation by making the unique redemptive sacrifice of Christ present in the eucharistic sacrifice of the church. Although all members of the community of believers participate in the one priesthood of Christ through their baptism, only men ordained to the priesthood "possess the authority to act in the power and place of the person of Christ himself" (no. 1548). In the person of the bishop or priest, "the presence of Christ is made visible in the midst of the community of believers" and finds its fullness of meaning when the priest celebrates the eucharistic sacrifice. This is not a merely symbolic power made visible in the person of the priest but a real power "which is none other than that of Christ" (no. 1551). And only men can be ordained because the "Lord Jesus chose only men to form the college of the twelve apostles, and the apostles did the same when they chose collaborators to succeed them in their ministry" (no. 1577). Therefore, the Catholic Church is not authorized to admit women to holy orders. And, in the Latin Rite, priests are "normally chosen from among men of faith who live a celibate life and who intend to remain celibate" (no. 1579). These, then, are the men through whom "Christ acts and effects salvation" (no. 1584). As the *Catechism* tersely puts it, "[t]he grace of the Holy Spirit proper to this sacrament is configuration to Christ as Priest, Teacher and Pastor of whom the ordained is made a minister" (no. 1585).

This translates, for most Catholics, into five major points. The priest is the local representative of the church hierarchy, and as such has authority to decide how the parish will operate—financially and pastorally. While laypeople may be and sometimes are consulted, they have no real decision-making power. Secondly, the priest speaks for God and the church when he preaches from the pulpit, when he admonishes in the confessional or counsels in spiritual direction; he expresses the will of God and therefore must be obeyed. Thirdly, the priest has the "sacred power," the power of Christ himself, to make God present and active in our lives through the sacraments, most notably through the sacrifice of Eucharist. And so it is through the sacraments of the church, administered by the priest, that Catholics have access to God. It is through the sacraments, confession in particular, that spiritual experiences and issues related to conscience and morality come under the priest's scrutiny. A corollary to this is that the Holy Spirit works mainly, if not exclusively, through the church's sacramental ministry. Fourth, priests are celibate: ordained men don't have sexual relationships and married men are not allowed to be ordained (unless they are "converting" from another Christian church and want to retain their clerical status). Finally, women cannot be admitted to holy orders. This may seem a gross oversimplification of the faith of ordinary Catholics, particularly of Catholic women. But in my interviews and conversations with abused women, many of whom were vowed religious, this is basically how they perceive the priest's power and role in their lives. Such a perception of the priesthood, of course, presents several problems.

THE PRIEST'S POSITION OF LEADERSHIP

The first problem has to do with the prestige attached to the priesthood. Priests rank higher on the social, and certainly on the ecclesial scale, than laypeople. Besides, as one priest puts it,

> they are educated, fairly articulate, and have decent social skills. They are typically self-possessed and most often present themselves pretty well. They are usually competent at what they do. . . . Priests are also mysterious, fascinating. They are typically spiritual people, perceived as holy. The priest holds esoteric power and is regarded as having knowledge about the spiritual realm and wisdom about life. Most priests know the innermost secrets of many around them. They also hold a position of leadership that offers them real power to inspire people's minds and hearts.[3]

Catholic women in general, even women who are sexually abused, harassed, or exploited by a priest, hold the clergy in very high regard. In fact, sometimes their reverence borders on adulation. Their greatest fear seems to be displeasing the priest not only because he represents God but because, in this capacity, he is an important person in the community. Their families or religious congregation take pride in the fact that "Father" has enough consideration for them to count them as personal friends—which gives them a greater sense of worth. This valuation from the outside is consistent with the lack of true self-esteem and need to please of the codependent person we saw earlier. The only value some Catholics see in themselves is that which the clergy deigns to bestow on them. Janet's story illustrates this.

One of several victims of the same parish priest, Janet became sexually involved with her pastor at a time of profound grief: her husband and only daughter had both died in an automobile accident. James, her pastor, claimed she needed physical intimacy with a man to help her forget her huge loss. After nearly three years, Janet severed the relationship when she discovered James was also "comforting" other widows in the parish in the same way. Instead of reporting James to his bishop, Janet confided in another priest under the seal of confession what had happened and made him promise not to report James to the bishop. The reason? Both the bishop and her confessor had close personal ties to her family and she would not risk losing the bishop's respect but also the vicarious prestige of having a person as important as the bishop as a friend. So, while she now calls James a "scumbag," she refuses to take part in any action against him—for fear of being perceived by the clergy as a "tramp and a troublemaker." When her name finally did come up in another woman's complaint, the bishop called to ask her if this was true and how could he help. He had been very supportive at the time that she lost her husband and daughter, but she was now so ashamed that she had fallen prey to a sexual predator that she felt unworthy of his pastoral concern.

It is this same reverence for the clergy that prompts many women to work in parishes or diocesan offices. Most of the time they are underpaid, overworked, and can be dismissed at the whim of the pastor or bishop. Working for the priest, in their minds, is the same as working for the Lord and it is their way of furthering the mission of the church. Marcella was one such woman. She gave up a thriving retail business to become parish secretary. After some years, a new pastor was appointed. It took Marcella little time to realize that the parish, or more precisely the pastor, was living above his means, spending huge amounts on books, courses, retreats and holidays, all in the interest of Father Fred's "personal growth." When Marcella told him the parish bank account was overdrawn, he ignored her. Marcella then raised the issue at a parish council meeting where she served as treasurer. Fred dismissed her remarks by saying he was entitled to continue his priestly formation in any way he saw fit and that, in any case, it was really not her place to question his decisions. Later that week, he fired Marcella, telling the parish council that she was incompetent, and perhaps not too honest. No one dared contradict the pastor. When Marcella wrote to her bishop to complain of the unjustified dismissal, she received a written reply from the diocesan head of finance saying the pastor suspected her of embezzling parish funds. Privately, however, the diocesan official told her he knew from past experience that Father Fred had expensive tastes, so the diocese was prepared to forget the allegation, "forgive" Marcella, and allow her to work in a neighboring parish, but without signing authority. When asked why she accepted the job, she answered that she needed the work because her family's business had taken a downturn. When a lawyer offered to sue the diocese on her behalf at his expense, she refused, saying, "It just wouldn't be proper to take the church to court."

Both Marcella and Janet not only exhibit all the characteristics of clergy codependence described earlier, but also the sense of inferiority many women feel with regard to men, especially clergy. As we shall see in the next chapter, much of this sense of inferiority comes from the understanding women have internalized of their nature and role in life and in the church. It must be said, on the other hand, that for many women, being unjustly dismissed from their church work was an awareness-raising event. They suddenly realized that part of the problem was that they were not inferior—either in terms of intelligence, education, pastoral sense or dedication. In fact, women have often been dismissed for not accepting to be treated as inferior to men, even clergy. When they sought equality, they were labeled angry feminists and accused of simply wanting a share in the priest's power.

THE PRIEST'S SPIRITUAL POWER

The priest's spiritual power is very real and lies at the root of a second problem. When the priest is regarded as God's representative and mouthpiece, especially in confession and spiritual direction, he does have access to the most intimate details of a person's life—and knowledge is power. It is in confession and spiritual direction that we confront our authentic humanity with its frailties, weaknesses, needs, struggles, but also with its ideals, hopes, and dreams. And this is precisely the information a sexual predator can use to seduce his victims. It is also where women might express a desire to work for the church, discern a call to ministry or even the priesthood. More often than not, she will be encouraged to answer Christ's call to service by giving generously of her talents, time, and financial resources. It must be stated emphatically that in most cases, information gleaned in confession and spiritual direction is treated as sacred, as well it should. The fact that this sacred trust is abused speaks to the depravity of the abuser; it does not dispute the fact that ministers of the faith can be helpful witnesses to the mystery of God at work in another person's most intimate self. The problem arises when, instead of being a witness to grace, the priest substitutes himself for the Mystery and becomes a barrier to grace instead of a conduit. This is the "rape of the soul" that persons who have been abused by priests sometimes describe—and it is a far cry from the *Catechism* teaching that the priest's religious authority "must be measured against the model of Christ, who by love made himself the least and the servant of all."[4]

SACRIFICIAL PRIESTHOOD

Understanding the "sacred power" of the priesthood to offer the holy sacrifice of Eucharist is particularly problematic in that it establishes a clearly defined hierarchical structure, organized to ensure apostolic succession of a sacrificial priesthood and its associated continuity of power following a male lineage.[5] According to church teaching, sacrificial priesthood means that the priest offers, through the agency of bread and wine, the Body and Blood of Christ for the salvation of humanity. In doing so, the priest is not acting as an ordinary man, but supernaturally, in the person of Christ as a mediator between God and the faithful. This exclusive power to offer the Sacrifice of Mass is the foundation of hierarchical priestly authority, including the authority to speak for the church and make decisions. Laypeople must listen and obey. Even though this teaching was somewhat diluted by the Second Vatican Council when it highlighted the role of all the baptized in discerning the will of God for the church (the *sensus fidei*[6]), and many diocesan councils have been set up to consult the faithful laity, there is still a sense among many Catholics that the voice of the laity, women especially and their faith experience, have not been heard.[7] That's because the demarcation line between the clergy and the laity is the "sacred power" to preside over the sacrifice of Eucharist.

Sacrificial priesthood presents a further problem for women who have been abused by priests. The whole idea of this type of priesthood is based on a belief that God sent his only son into the world to be tortured and executed.[8] The danger of this understanding of the Incarnation is in depicting God as an angry father who *requires* the death of his son to atone for the sins of humanity. This belief is still prevalent among many Catholics who see Jesus as sacrificial "Lamb of God" rather than a flesh-and-blood, historically documented human being. They tend to not see Jesus as a real person whose love, compassion, mercy, and forgiveness were the embodiment of God; a healer who sided with sinners and the disenfranchised; a prophet who confronted the powerful and served as an example of personal power which was never harmful or hurtful to others. The majority of Catholic laity have not been educated in the faith as adults.

Consequently, when abused women begin to rethink their perception of the priest and the meaning of "sacrificial" religion, they rebel at the notion that there was some compulsion or obligation in God to sacrifice his son to save humanity. On the contrary, they come to regard the crucifixion of Jesus as they would all human suffering through the ages—God in Christ suffers with humanity. Part of their healing journey is in believing that Christ reaches out to the suffering, including women in the church who cannot speak for themselves. Christ helps them to name, confront, and resist the evil of abuse of power.

There is a further problem with an all-powerful Father–God who finds satisfaction in the "bloody sacrifice" of his Son dying for the crimes of others. Until this image of God is set aside, it will be very difficult to build a more just society or church. The problem here is believing that an innocent Jesus had to suffer at the hands of the powerful of his time *because God demanded it*. The biblical model invoked is Abraham sacrificing his son Isaac. This kind of literal interpretation forgets that, in the Bible story, God substituted a ram as the sacrificial offering, ending, one would hope, human sacrifices. More importantly for contemporary societies is the lesson taught, also in the Bible, that God wants justice for all; God hears the cries of the poor, the powerless, the vulnerable, and the helpless.

Moreover, when the priesthood is primarily associated with the power of offering the sacrifice of the Mass, a reversal takes place. Priestly power itself becomes the "sacred" reality. And as too often happens in hierarchical institutions, the powerful are entitled to many privileges that they want to maintain and that they can then abuse with impunity. That is the real problem with a hierarchical and sacrificial priesthood that dominates in official Roman Catholic teaching today, and which in effect takes precedence over the baptismal priesthood of all the faithful. It lends support to a system that exacts submission and blind obedience to a patriarchal and omnipotent God who is, in the final analysis, abusive. Images of such a God are still quite prevalent in Catholic liturgy, hymns, and devotions. The Precious Blood is invoked as the sacrifice that saves, intercedes, and seals the covenant of God with God's people. It forgets that what Jesus did was ask his disciples to break bread and lift the cup of wine in thanksgiving during a convivial meal, not a ritual sacrifice.

The idea of a priesthood based on the "sacred power" to celebrate the eucharistic sacrifice—offered to a bloodthirsty god—is even more problematic when the priest is identified with the saving Christ. The dynamic whereby a priest abuses his power, reenacting the drama of a godly patriarch who imposes obedience upon a son who is then sacrificed to save a sinful humanity, is the same dynamic as a priest abusing his victim, especially in cases of sexual abuse. When there is a sexual relationship between a priest and a parishioner, the pastoral role is reversed because the priest who is supposed to be bringing spiritual help and support is using a privileged relationship for his own sexual gratification. In other words, the priest substitutes himself for an almighty and abusive God and the victim takes on the role of Christ, assumes the sin of the priest, and submits to "the will of God," handing herself over body and soul to save a relationship upon which she has become dependent. This is not a consensual relationship between equals; it is an abuse of power, a relationship in which the love and justice of God and their power to heal and comfort have been twisted into a human sacrifice to the malevolence and manipulation of a sexual predator.

Historically speaking, of course, it was a cruel and oppressive political regime that crucified Jesus because he exposed it for what it was. In proposing the model of the Suffering Servant to the disciples of Christ, church teaching focuses on suffering as a form of retributive justice. This in turn has been invoked to encourage abused and battered women to accept sexual assault or exploitation as a form of redemptive suffering, to keep silent instead of naming the evil being done and confronting those who hurt them. Many of the women who spoke to me about having been sexually abused had been taught that in order to imitate Christ, they must accept, even choose, to suffer. They were convinced that if they offered up their lives for the priest, their suffering and silence would be redemptive both for themselves and the priest. Often, they identified with Christ offering up his life for others, and this encouraged them to forget themselves in favor of their abuser—who never had to face the consequences. The theology of priesthood as "sacred power" to offer the sacrifice of the Mass, which has been internalized by most Catholics, goes a long way to explain why some women "allow" themselves to be abused.

POWER DIFFERENTIAL AND CONSENT

The objection is sometimes raised that these women could have simply said no. This indicates a serious misunderstanding of meaningful consent. When a priest engages in sexual activity with a member of his parish, for instance, it is a case of abuse of power, not consensual sexual activity, because the woman involved, whether through naiveté, social conditioning, or religious upbringing, still views the priest as God's representative. This gives the priest an almost immeasurable amount of power. The power differential is obvious: he is theologically better educated, invested with a "sacred power" to be a channel of God's grace through the sacraments, and is a respected member of the community whose advice is sought by others. He is called to lead the community in worship and is perceived as an exemplar of Christian moral living. In reality, however, the pastor who sexually abuses a parishioner is no different from a secular sex offender:

He is manipulative, coercive, controlling, predatory, and sometimes violent. He may also be charming, bright, competent, and
charismatic. He is attracted to powerlessness and vulnerability.
He is not psychotic, but is usually sociopathic; that is, he has
little or no sense of conscience about his offending behaviors. He
usually will minimize, lie, and deny when confronted.[9]

Very often the pastor may have a greater degree of financial
security and the ability to reward or punish. This was seen to be
the case in Africa, for instance, where priests who "traditionally
would have sought out prostitutes" instead turned to secondary
school girls and nuns because they were considered "safe" from
HIV according to the report presented to the Congregation for
Institutes of Consecrated Life and Societies of Apostolic Life, the
Vatican office that oversees religious life.[10] The report goes on to
say that "sexual harassment and even rape of sisters by priests
and bishops is allegedly common, and that sometimes when a
sister becomes pregnant, the priest insists that she have an abortion." Women in developing countries are "socially conditioned
to be subservient to men," the report states. It would be fair to
say that all women in the church have been conditioned to regard themselves as inferior to priests because they can only be
mere members of the laity, and as such are to accept the priest's
dictates as the will of God in their lives, and comply with his
wishes. And so, they obey.

THE MEANING OF CELIBACY

It would seem, continues the *National Catholic Reporter*, that in
some cultures where celibacy is not valued, "a priest does not
get married but that does not mean he does not have children"
or that he is expected to "embrace celibacy freely and . . . publicly manifest their intention of staying celibate for the love of
God's kingdom. . . ."[11] The difference in perception of celibacy
is not only found in the Third World. Consider the story of a Canadian woman I'll call Frances. She had been in a religious order
for almost twenty years when she became sexually involved with

the pastor of the parish where she headed the liturgy committee. It began one day in the confessional when George, the priest,
asked her if she had difficulty with sexual fantasies. When she
said she sometimes did, George told her that having sex would
be the best way of dealing with these troublesome feelings. In
fact, he said, she should ask to be relieved of her vow of chastity,
which meant leaving her community. She asked her superiors
for a leave of absence from the community, during which time
she went on a holiday with George. They shared the same room.
When Frances asked George how he reconciled what they were
doing with his promise of celibacy, he told her, "I promised not
to get married, not to abstain from sex." Their relationship went
on for several months during which Frances lived outside her
community. She finally asked to be released from her vows, expecting George would do the same so they could marry. George
replied that he could never do that, flew into a fit of rage, beat
and raped her. Frances later discovered that two other women in
the parish were "sleeping" with George, so she reported him to
the bishop. George admitted to his bishop that he had a problem
with celibacy and requested to be sent to a treatment center for
sexual addiction. It was only when Frances threatened the diocese to go to the police that George was removed from active
priestly ministry.

Priests who abuse their "sacred power" claim they have a
greater knowledge of God and the truth. This is not surprising in
view of the fact that the teaching authority of the church whom
they represent claims to be infallible and therefore incapable of
error when it comes to discerning the will of Christ and the real
needs of Catholics.[12] All faithful Catholics are expected to submit
to that authority. Following the same pattern, abusive priests tell
their victims that they know what celibacy is really about, they
know what is best for their flock, and many women have accepted this at great personal cost.

The harm done to these women is seldom acknowledged.
Like many secular organizations, the institutional church hes-

itates and even refuses to place responsibility squarely on the shoulders of the guilty party. Many times women have been told that they seduced the priest, a "good" and "holy" man. Others have been persuaded not to lodge a complaint because the priest was "a man of prayer" who "would never do such a thing." Admitting that priests have their weaknesses and are sinners like all human beings would allow responsibility to be assigned where it belongs: with the abusing priest and not the victim. Absolving the priest of any responsibility and protecting him with a cloak of secrecy and a conspiracy of silence, ignoring the abuse by passing it off as an "indiscretion" or "poor judgment" is tantamount to tacit approval. This is yet another form of abuse that perpetuates violence as acceptable, both in the church and in society as a whole. This also means that the priest is not held responsible before God, his victim, or his parish community. He becomes "untouchable" and the sin falls on the woman "seductress."

The abusive priest is protected by the institution, transferred to another parish to avoid creating a scandal. Lay Catholics have no voice or official recourse within the church institution, and even though more and more dioceses now have policies to deal with allegations of sexual misconduct or harassment, these policies are not always enforced. Of the women I interviewed in the course of my research, most felt they were not believed, or worse, had been further victimized by the investigation process—which was in all cases conducted by a diocesan official or a major superior of a religious community, almost always a priest. The women did not understand why their bishop, who is their spiritual leader as well as the offending priest's, did not come to their defense. Consequently, when it came to dispensing justice, the scales invariably tipped on the priest's side: he is a member of the hierarchy, invested with "sacred power"; women are members of the laity, relegated to the secular domain. This would explain why the women who have the financial resources to do so, though they are few, seek some form of justice in the civil courts.

For many women trying to rebuild their lives after an abuse of power, the experience can be a consciousness-raising about their oppressed status within the church. The women who shared their stories of clergy exploitation with me admitted they considered leaving the church because of the way they had been treated. Some did leave because they saw it as hopelessly patriarchal and unwilling to change. They refused to be treated as second-class human beings. Others, believing that they too are the church, mobilized to work for change, joining reform movements, less structured base communities, or small house churches. They stay in the hope of finding a place within the Catholic fold where they could celebrate their faith without feeling "schizophrenic"—not in the clinical sense, of course, but rather of being of two minds, wanting to stay in the Catholic Church but feeling oppressed within it and having nowhere else to go.

The perception of the priest as embodiment of Christ is severely questioned by women who have been sexually abused or harassed. The abuse of power they have suffered is particularly perverse because it betrays everything Jesus came to teach and exemplify. It can be helpful to remind them that Jesus knew to what degree power tends to corrupt[13] and become tyrannical, especially when it is religious power that claims to come from God. And so, when women question the "sacred power" of the sacrificial priesthood, it is not so much that they reject the idea that Christ accepted to die for them, or that the Eucharist re-enacts Christ's sacrifice. It is rather that abused and exploited women have difficulty finding healing in the Eucharist when it is presided by a man they know to be a sexual predator or a spiritual tyrant. The Eucharist could become a source of healing for them if it were true to its original meaning: thanksgiving to God in Christ who came to free humanity from sin and oppression. But that would require a renewal in the church's understanding of the priesthood. It would also call for a process of reconciliation that seldom takes place because the priest, in almost all cases, has been advised either by his bishop or his bishop's lawyers not to acknowledge that he has sinned, much less ask for forgiveness.

ONLY MEN CAN BE PRIESTS

It is disturbing to observe the impact a sacrificial type of ministerial priesthood has had on the lives of all Catholic women. "Sacred power" has been used and abused to drive a wedge between women and their faith. The experience of women who have been abused by clergy raises some serious questions regarding the consistently maintained doctrine that the male hierarchical model of church is a divine institution entrusted with the salvation of all humanity. Is this kind of "sacred power" willed by God? Was the patriarchal and hierarchical institution we have today instituted this way by Jesus Christ? Was it Christ's intention that only men would have access to the "sacred power" received at holy orders to teach, govern, and sanctify through the administration of the sacraments, especially the eucharistic sacrifice? Considering the damage caused by a literal and legalistic understanding of a "sacred" hierarchical and sacrificial priesthood, it is not surprising many Catholics have come to the conclusion that current church teaching on the priesthood needs serious reconsideration. This paradigm of priesthood supports a system that allows for the abuse of clerical power and is discriminatory toward all women.

Nonetheless, many Catholic women, even among those who have experienced sexual abuse, harassment, and unfair dismissal from church work, perceive the priesthood as a male prerogative—this is, after all, the teaching of the church—and in maintaining this teaching, is the pope not infallible? They couldn't understand why John Paul II's letter prohibiting the admission of women to holy orders[14] had touched a nerve in so many Catholics. It was only when they sought counseling to cope with their spiritual distress that many sexually abused women began to wish they could confide in a woman who had the "sacred power" of the sacraments at her disposal to nurture and heal their damaged souls. Some, of course, turned to professional therapists and ordained women in other denominations. This got them wondering why, exactly, women could not be priests. The more theologically literate among them allowed themselves to question the teaching, and read the papal document with new eyes. The first thing they notice in John Paul's letter on the non-admission of women to holy orders is that it is addressed to the venerable brothers in the episcopate, not to women themselves. Not addressing people directly about matters that concern them convinces women that they are not only second-class citizens in the church, but actually invisible in the minds of their church leaders. As one very sympathetic priest told me, "You (women) aren't even on the Vatican radar screen."

It is no coincidence that it was only when other Christian denominations began ordaining women that some of them, as ordained ministers, began to denounce abuses they had suffered themselves. By speaking out, they allowed other women to come forward and seek justice for the harm that had been done to them by clergymen. It would seem that as long as women are not admitted to the ordained priesthood, they will have no credibility and no voice within the hierarchical structure of the Catholic Church. Consequently, church officials, with a few exceptions, will see no need to address the evil of clergy sexual misconduct and abuse of power. The refusal to admit women to holy orders is inconsistent with compelling archeological evidence to the contrary—in the early church women were deacons, priests, and even bishops. Why would the church refuse to acknowledge this and the fact that the Spirit is moving in the lives of the innumerable Catholic women, if not to consolidate the sacred power of the priesthood in the hands of men? This thought led many women who had progressed in their journey of recovery from clergy codependence to suspect that there is an addiction to power at work among church authorities very similar to that exercised by priests who abused their authority over them. And women are powerless to change the system because they are not part of the decision-making process of the system. Indeed, the description of addiction proposed by Anne Wilson Schaef seems to apply to the dynamic of power at work within the hierarchy of the Catholic Church:

> An addiction is any process over which we are powerless. It takes control of us, causing us to do and think things that are inconsistent with our personal values and leading us to become progressively more compulsive and obsessive. A sure sign of an addiction is the sudden need to deceive ourselves and others—to lie, deny, and cover up. An addiction is anything we feel *tempted* to lie about. An addiction is anything we are not *willing* to give up.[15]

In their search for healing and wholeness, many abused Catholic women had to be willing to give up not only their dependence on the clergy to have access to the sacred, but also a certain image and understanding of themselves.

Readings

For a better understanding of the Catholic priesthood, I recommend Michael L. Papesh, *Clerical Culture: Contradiction and Transformation* (Collegeville: Liturgical Press, 2004). It provides a readable history of the clerical state and some of the problems it faces today. About the dynamic of power at work within the church, its impact on the clergy and on clergy–laity relationships, see Michael H. Crosby, *The Dysfunctional Church: Addiction and Codependency in the Family of Catholicism* (Notre Dame, IN: Ave Maria Press, 1991) as well as the other books quoted in this chapter.

For those who wish to explore a model of faith based on friendship rather than sacrifice, I recommend Elisabeth Moltmann-Wendel, "Friendship—The Forgotten Category for Faith and Christian Community" in Jürgen Moltmann and Elisabeth Moltmann-Wendel, *Passion for God: Theology in Two Voices* (Louisville, KY: Westminster John Knox Press, 2003).

Notes

1. Michael L. Papesh, *Clerical Culture, Contradiction and Transformation* (Collegeville: Liturgical Press, 2004) 19.

2. *Catechism of the Catholic Church* (New York: Doubleday, 1994) 1.

3. Papesh, *Clerical Culture*, 96–97.

4. *Catechism of the Catholic Church*, no. 1551.

5. N. Jay, *Throughout Your Generations Forever* (Chicago: University of Chicago Press, 1992) 112.

6. *Catechism of the Catholic Church*, nos. 904–911.

7. See Mary Catherine Hilkert, *Experience and Tradition: Can the Center Hold?* In C. M. LaCugna, ed., *Freeing Theology* (HarperSanFrancisco, 1993) 74–76.

8. This could be one interpretation of several Scripture passages. See "CHRIST OFFERED HIMSELF TO HIS FATHER FOR OUR SINS," *Catechism of the Catholic Church*, nos. 606–609.

9. Marie M. Fortune, *Is Nothing Sacred?* (Cleveland: United Church Press, 1999) 47.

10. John L. Allen Jr. and Pamela Schaeffer, "Reports of Abuse: AIDS Exacerbates Sexual Exploitation of Nuns," *National Catholic Reporter*, March 16, 2001.

11. *Catechism of the Catholic Church*, no. 1599.

12. Surprisingly few "Catholics in the pew" realize that papal infallibility dates back only to Pius IX and the First Vatican Council of the 1870s. In spite of its provocative title, a very readable account of this is found in historian Garry Wills's book, *Papal Sin: Structures of Deceit* (New York: Doubleday, 2000) 246–259.

13. See Mark 10:42-45 and Matthew 20:20-28 where Jesus cautions his disciples about "lording it over" others.

14. John Paul II, "*Ordinatio Sacerdotalis*, Apostolic Letter on Ordination and Women," *Origins*, Vol. 24, No. 4, 1994.

15. A. W. Schaef, *When Society Becomes an Addict*, 18.

Chapter 4

CATHOLIC WOMEN'S REALITY

Women who have suffered an abuse of power in the church do not initially see themselves as powerless victims of an oppressive religious system. Yet the fact remains that within the Catholic Church women are powerless to effect any change at an institutional level because they have no voice in formulating doctrine or church law. Because women are kept silent and invisible, they are neither at the altar nor the pulpit. It is therefore not surprising that they have been assigned an image and an understanding of themselves not based on their own experience. Their very nature, their gender specificity, and their role in the church and in society, are carefully laid out in official church teaching, crafted by a centuries-long line of popes, theologians, biblical scholars, liturgists, and canon lawyers, all of whom were men.

Lynn, whose story follows below, is representative of several women who have come to workshops and retreats for women abused by clergy to make the point that there is a system at work within the church that affects the lives of all women. Sexual assault and unjustified dismissal from church employment are not the only ways priests and bishops abuse their power.

LYNN'S STORY

Lynn grew up in a devoutly Catholic family. Her parents were farmers. She, her two sisters, and her brother were educated in Catholic schools and attended Mass every Sunday, sometimes even weekdays during Lent, as was the custom in their small community. Lynn wanted to be a nurse when she grew up, but had to find a job as soon as she finished high school because her parents couldn't afford to pay for her training as a nurse. She moved to the city, found a job, and a new parish. There she met and married Rick. Very early in the marriage, she realized Rick was an alcoholic and had a bad temper. As the children began to arrive, he also became increasingly violent. After a particularly vicious beating, Lynn went to confession to seek the advice of her pastor. He told her to go home and have sex with her husband as often as she physically could. After Rick had severely beaten up their nine-year-old daughter, Lynn confided in her pastor that she was considering leaving her husband. He told her that marriage is a sacrament of the church; it confers upon her all the graces she needed to endure her suffering; that she was being extremely selfish; and he refused to give her absolution if she did not change her mind. Lynn, who said all she ever wanted was to be a good Christian wife and mother, left her husband and no longer considers herself a Catholic. She told her story to our support group to make the point that priests also abuse their spiritual power when they shame women into staying in abusive marriages. When asked where she saw God in all of this, she said she had no idea where even to begin looking for God.

Lynn was told she would be refused the sacraments if she didn't stay in an abusive marriage. Other women told us of being turned away from Communion or of losing their teaching positions in Catholic schools because they were divorced. Still others were ostracized by their community because they had applied for an annulment after many years of struggling to raise their families alone, yet it was the husband who had abandoned the marriage. The most painful were the stories of the women who were told they were jeopardizing their eternal salvation for leaving an abusive husband—whose violence ranged from financial and emotional abuse to beatings and death threats. Their witness provides valuable insight into the understanding women have of themselves when their consciences are controlled by an all-male clergy. It points to a systemic problem in an androcentric religion—one that keeps women silent and invisible at the institutional level and vulnerable targets of violence at the personal level.

These voices need to be heard. They also need a faith community that accepts listening to them without judging in order to rekindle and nourish a faith that had been betrayed. They are the ones who see most clearly the systemic abuses at work within the Catholic Church because it mirrors their experience of living in a repressive and abusive relationship. They are keenly aware of the unquestioned authority male figures have had in their lives. Not only pastors, but male doctors and lawyers, for instance, were considered by their mothers and teachers as more knowledgeable and reliable than their female counterparts. Questioning this traditional view meant exposing oneself to rejection within the family, cutting oneself off from a much-needed support system. Just as in the larger society, it is very difficult for Catholic women to walk away from an abusive marriage, especially if the husband has the support and blessing, tacit or explicit, of the church's representative. In the church, as in other patriarchal societies and institutions, men are reluctant to give up the power that gives them control over women's minds and bodies.

Women who freed themselves from a violent domestic situation and have gone on to lead meaningful, satisfying, and productive lives describe a series of myths that shaped their self-image and self-understanding. They are grounded in Catholic tradition and are even more firmly entrenched than the codependence characteristics we saw earlier.

WOMAN AS OCCASION OF SIN

Women have heard from time immemorial that sin came into the world because of Eve. It was she who first gave in to the tempter and dragged her mate into disobedience. How this translates in modern times is that women are to blame for the moral transgressions of men. Many women remember being told, as teenagers, that if they "kept their place," boys would keep a respectful and chaste distance. Proposed as model of adolescent chastity is St. Maria Goretti, who preferred to die rather than lose her virginity. The double-bind for women is that they are both the cause and victim of men's "lower" instincts.

Because they have internalized the notion that they are an occasion of sin for men, women exhibit an existential form of guilt and shame turned against themselves when they suffer some form of violence. How many rape victims blame themselves for what happened? How often has it been said, "She really wanted it, even when she said no"? How many little girls have been victims of rape and incest simply because "they were just too sexy"? A corollary to this is that female beauty—even that of a young child—is demonized, justifying women being beaten into submission. And how many battered women excuse their partner's violent behavior because they believe they deserved it?

WOMAN AS SEXUAL OBJECT

Women are further fed the myth that men have sexual "needs," meaning they cannot live without sex,[1] whereas women, with the exception of prostitutes, are inclined to be naturally chaste, meaning they have no natural sex drive. One manifestation of this notion is that women's sexual needs appear nowhere in the Vatican-sanctioned "rhythm method" of family planning that involves abstaining from sexual intercourse when the woman is fertile. That this coincides with when a woman is most intensely aroused sexually is of no consequence because of the myth that virtuous women have no sexual impulses. The whore vs. virgin dualism in Catholic understanding of human nature is widespread and pervasive, to the point that sensual pleasure is always somewhat suspect—particularly in devout Catholic women—and completely incompatible with intimacy with God and holiness of life.

The vast majority of women in the industrialized world do not practice "natural family planning." Not that the encyclical *Humanae Vitae*,[2] forbidding all forms of artificial contraception, was initially intended to protect the health and well-being of women; it was rather seen by women and many men as a refusal by the Vatican authorities to grant married couples, and women in particular, any kind of moral agency in matters of sexuality and reproduction. Closer to us, and to the shame of the policymakers in the Vatican, women are dying in horrific numbers from AIDS because the church won't allow the use of condoms. "Artificial contraception," with the notable exception of the condom and vasectomy, revolves around women's fertility, which lasts for approximately twenty-four hours every twenty-eight days, for thirty to forty years of a woman's life, whereas most men are fertile all the time, from puberty often into old age. The diaphragm to prevent fertilization, the contraceptive pill to prevent ovulation, the uterine coil to prevent implantation, abortion to destroy the fetus, tubal ligation to permanently prevent fertilization, the morning-after pill to prematurely trigger the menstrual cycle, and on down the list, all rest squarely on the shoulders of women[3] and are not without serious implications for their health. Yet many women take these risks because of a deep-seated belief that it is their duty to meet their husband's sexual needs, but also not to get pregnant because he has the right to decide how many children are enough.

WOMAN AS OBEDIENT CHILD

Women in abusive relationships have been socialized to believe that they are intellectually inferior to men, and so they should defer to men's authority. Unquestioning, almost blind obedience, rather than critical thinking, was inculcated in all the victims of domestic and clergy violence I interviewed. Even if what the priest demanded went counter to their conscience or better judgment, these women felt strongly pressured to conform their behavior to the priest's judgment rather than trust their own instincts, intuition, common sense, and experience. As we saw earlier, by virtue of his sacred power, the priest is credited with having a superior knowledge of God's will, and what women need to do to save their immortal souls. Moral agency and autonomous critical thinking are simply not part of the equation. Obedience to the priest was inculcated at home where parental authority, also from God by virtue of the fourth commandment to "honor thy father and mother," is a derived form of religious authority rooted in obedience to the church in the person of the parish priest. Obedience was further re-inforced at school, especially in Catholic schools, where nuns taught the dogmas and doctrines of the faith under the spiritual authority of the priest—to whom they always deferred. Taught from the cradle to be obedient daughters, women were warned to be wary of feminism—both in the church and society as a whole—because it was nothing less than open rebellion against God's design for humanity. One of the inevitable consequences, of course, is to keep women permanently infantile and therefore dependent on men to make all decisions for them—including what they should think and believe about themselves.

Here, as in what we saw earlier about women's understand-ing of the faith, the church, and the priesthood, I can hear pro-tests that this is a cruel caricature of women's sense of self, certainly not derived from Catholic teaching on women. It could even be argued that the church promotes and defends the hu-man rights of women. For instance, Mulieris Dignitatem,[4] a medi-tation John Paul II addressed to all Catholics on the occasion of the last Marian Year, was ostensibly written to promote the dignity and vocation of women. In it, the late Pope reminds us that woman, like man, is created in the image of God. Her first mission is to be a helpmate for man in procreation, as wife and mother,[5] fully equal in terms of humanity. Then, in an attempt to rectify the misconception that it was through Eve alone that sin came into the world, the point is made that "women are not more responsible for sin than men," and moreover that union with God, the source of a mutual relationship between men and women, was broken by the "sin of the human being."[6] Nonethe-less, the consequence of sin would be heavier to bear for women, particularly regarding the domination of men over them. This "indicates the disturbance and loss of stability of that fundamental equality which men and women possess" and is a violation of it. Women cannot, in seeking liberation from this domination, aspire to appropriate male characteristics contrary to their own feminine "originality," for then they would "lose what constitutes their essential richness."[7]

To underscore the fact that women are full partners in God's plan for the world, John Paul II reminds us that "God addresses himself directly to women" in Scripture[8] because women "from the beginning inherit the dignity of personhood—and Jesus makes it part of the Gospel."[9] The Gospel innovation is that "in the relationship between husband and wife, the 'subjection' is not one-sided but mutual."[10]

What John Paul II does in *Mulieris Dignitatem* is propose Mary as a model to women, a model of submission. And rather than speak in terms of true equality, the Pope prefers to speak in terms of complementarity both in roles and in functions, meaning that women are by nature called to help men fulfill their roles and functions. Mary is not portrayed as an equal partner, nor as a mature and autonomous adult. Rather, she is an idealized woman portrayed as virgin, mother, and chaste spouse, the protective shield for the overvaluation of virginity and a safety valve for priestly celibacy. This is what is really holy about her—the ideal of sexual morality. Women have a role different from men. They are to mother children—biologically or spiritually—and transmit to them the faith and tradition of the church. John Paul II insists that women are not inferior to men, not even to priests. Women have an even greater mission than that of the priesthood, and that is to follow the example of Mary, who is symbolically superior because she answered to perfection the call to humble service.[11]

This is a subtle ploy—overvaluing symbolic womanhood while at the same time refusing to grant woman full human status. Women who are familiar with dysfunctional systems easily see through this strategy. The women who described to me their experiences of abuse admitted they were fooled by this at first, and some were admittedly flattered, but they eventually realized that compliments (overvaluing) usually came with a request for even more service. As A. W. Schaef suggests, "There is no group in our society more adept at this process than the church, for which one of the major premises is that of eternal life. That promise keeps us actively involved in pleasing the church and doing what it tells us to."[12] Indeed, the Pope attributes to women a greater dignity, but assigns them to a lower status: men are created to command, women to obey. Nowhere is this more accurately symbolized than in Catholic liturgies. Men are vested in the insignia of power in the sanctuary (front, center, and usually elevated), while women sit, watch, listen, and respond from the pew. Women are told how virtuous, loving, and compassionate they can be, and that by demonstrating these qualities in everyday life, they are fulfilling their vocation in the eyes of God.

What is disheartening is that the life and faith experience of women is not recorded or taken into account since they have taken no active part in the church's defining of their nature, their reality, their mission, or their special gifts. The myths that women have internalized reflect a centuries-old attitude among the clergy that the oppression and domination of women, while sinful, is to be endured rather than denounced.

The difficulty with this understanding of women and the roles of women, both in the church and in society, is that the Vatican's Congregation for the Doctrine of the Faith calls the church "expert in humanity"[13] without ever giving voice or lending credence to half the world's population. This may explain the discrepancy between the teaching that men and women are equal and its application in real life. On the one hand, it claims that women are responsible with men for the common destiny of humanity, but when women want to change the structures that contribute to their oppression, they are accused of power-mongering. "Faced with the abuse of power, the answer for women is to seek power."[14] Clearly, there is a misunderstanding here. The hierarchy seems to understand power as lording over, while women understand power as capacity to effect change. True dialogue could help clear up this misconception. In the meantime, the church hierarchy closes women's access to positions of real authority at the institutional level and can dismiss at will those women who, because of their competence and personal commitment, have come to acquire a considerable degree of authority and influence. Yet, when these women are asked why they dedicate so much of their gifts and energy to the service of the church and its people, they invariably answer that, as disciples, they try to be as open as possible to the Spirit, using the gifts God gave them, in Christ and through Christ. And even though the discussion on the ordination of women was officially ended by the Vatican, many Catholics still ask: if God gives gifts of leadership to women, and if some women believe God is calling them to the priesthood, why can they not also act "in the person of Christ"?

The problem is that John Paul's lofty vision of womanhood described in *Mulieris Dignitatem* did not trickle down to the seminaries. Women are still not understood as mature, autonomous, and fully equal in human terms in the consciousness of most priests because the majority of them are older men. Many still believe that only the priest is vested with the sacred power to act in the person of Christ and give access, through the sacraments of the church, to the realm of God.

EXCLUDED FROM THE REALM OF THE SACRED

I said earlier that there is, in dysfunctional systems, a tendency to distort the truth. Is it really true that the perpetual immaturity of women and their dependence on a hierarchical clergy in the order of grace is God's will? The teaching authority of the church maintains that only the male priest can act in the person of Christ. Sacramentally becoming Jesus Christ, the priest acts, not in his human capacity, but as intermediary between God and God's people. It is sometimes astonishing to hear the numbers of abused women who believe that access to the realm of the sacred comes only through the sacraments or the priest.

When asked to describe their spiritual life, we discover that it boils down to following the advice of their pastor: "Attend Mass as often as possible and take Communion. Come to confession regularly and frequently. Pray the rosary daily." Taking Communion would soothe their troubled soul and fortify them to put up with whatever suffering life reserved them. Examination of conscience in preparation for confession consists of reviewing their failings, taking full responsibility for them, and resolving to make amends. These women were not encouraged to cultivate, through meditation or reading of Scripture, a deep inner (as opposed to public or vocal) life of prayer. In view of the testimonies of women who freed themselves from abusive relationships and went on to heal their battered spirits and bodies, it seems no coincidence that women who did pursue different avenues of spirituality, even if they abandoned the practice of the sacraments, managed to recover their physical, emotional, and spiritual well-being. They had found their own access road to the sacred Divine.

Conversely, the women who seem most irretrievably "stuck" in the posture of victims and unhealthy lifestyles are most reluctant to seek spiritual help from anyone who isn't a priest. They shy away from spiritual advisors, psychologists, or psychiatrists who probe too deeply into their "soul" because matters of conscience should be dealt with only in sacramental confession. They categorically refuse to consider meditation as a form of prayer. In conversation with them, it becomes apparent that they cannot allow themselves to deal with the anger they carry inside—first because anger is one of the deadly sins and secondly because their anger must never be directed at a priest because he is "another Christ." The unfortunate result is that some never get the help they need. Others, fortunately, were finally advised by their pastor or confessor to seek professional counseling. As we shall see further on, professional help is what starts many women on their journey to wholeness.

The notion that only the ordained male has access to the sacred and can act in Christ's name, that only they can speak for the church hierarchy who knows the will of Christ, is alienating for all laypeople, not only women. It implies that the Spirit of Christ is not really active in all the members of God's people. Taken literally, this would mean that divine grace—God's presence and action through the Holy Spirit—is only accessible through the sacraments which in turn can only be celebrated by ordained men. Such a distortion and limiting of God is all the more alienating for women because it implies that they are incapable of experiencing intimacy with the Divine or especially to execute Christ-like actions, in particular the celebration of the Eucharist, simply because they do not have a man's body. Here again, women feel a double-bind, especially when they read the testimonies of women mystics. The truth that God is present in every person through the Holy Spirit, and that we are one in Christ (Gal 3:28), is what eventually sets these women free.

WHEN POWER BECOMES SACRED

Catholics understand the priest's vocation to mediate God to the faithful as a sacred power. It may prove useful to explore further the concept of power as a sacred reality to understand the impact its abuse can have. One dictionary definition of sacred is "associated with or dedicated to God; regarded with reverence because of this." More generally, though, we hold as "sacred" those values, objects, places, or persons that are touched by and signs of God's presence and activity. Religions establish sets of beliefs and rituals to make a distinction between the sacred and the secular, both in terms of objects and persons. To get to the fundamental problem in the issue of spiritual abuse by clergy, I believe we must consider the teaching of the church about holy orders in the light of these definitions.

As we saw earlier, the *Catholic Catechism* teaches that the sacrament of holy orders was instituted to endow celibate males with the power to offer the eucharistic sacrifice. Holy orders, then, creates an entirely new, exclusive class of persons set aside to sacramentally bring about the salvation of humanity. Women are allowed to take part in the sacrifice, but they cannot offer it because they do not have a body like that of Jesus who was male. Their only access to the sacred is through another person, the priest. But if it is mainly through the sacraments, Eucharist in particular, that God is present and active in building the church community, then women cannot be instruments of God's presence and action in the world. This would mean that God is limited to the sacramental actions of ordained ministers. And yet, the *Catechism*, quoting 2 Corinthians 5:17-18, also says that "the Grace of Christ is the gratuitous gift that God makes to us of his own life, infused by the Holy Spirit into our soul to heal it of sin and to sanctify it" (no. 1999). This apparent inconsistency can only be explained if the sacrament of holy orders was actually instituted to maintain hierarchical power, which raises a fundamental question: who determines the locus of God's presence and divine action, the hierarchy or the Holy Spirit? The inconsistency can perhaps also be explained by the intent of different teachings. I alluded to the circular arguments used by the magisterium to justify giving only bishops and priests the right to teach, govern, and sanctify in God's name. That comes very close to claiming to *be* God when it comes time to establish church law. But when the church uses a more scriptural language, there appears the mysteriously active and sanctifying presence known as the Spirit who "blows where it wills" and who teaches Christ's disciples "all things" (see John 3:8 and 14:26).

One of the major problems for all women in the church today is that they have no part in decision-making, whether it's on doctrinal, liturgical, or moral issues, and that exclusion has become encoded in canon law. By constantly invoking this legal construct, rather than sound theological and scriptural arguments, the hierarchy keeps itself in power. In the process, it loses sight of the fact that God is Mystery, and that the sacred is not an exclusive fortress to be protected and defended by the rule of law. Rather, the sacred is a constantly widening reality called to extend to all creation that tells the wonders of God and is called to be consecrated by humanity to its Creator. The more we try to limit the boundaries of the sacred—understood as touched by divine presence and action—the more it will elude us. In other words, by obstinately holding on to its exclusively legalistic understanding of "sacred power" and excluding women from it at all costs, church authorities are in effect using canon law to quench the Spirit.

Another reality that has been given sacred status is the current church teaching on women. John Paul II, as we have seen, says that the non-admission of women to ordination cannot mean that they are of "lesser dignity, nor can it be construed as discrimination against them."[15] It is based on the traditional teaching, also to be held as "absolute truth," that while women and men are equal in dignity, women have a special nature "essentially different"[16] from men's. This prompts Rosemary Radford Ruether to write that

> Christianity inherits from its historical past a fundamental contradiction in its views and treatment of one half of humanity, women. On the one hand Christianity, from its beginnings, has committed itself to a universalist soteriological egalitarianism. All human beings, regardless of gender, class, or ethnicity, are created by God and saved by Christ. Salvation knows no distinction between human beings. On the other hand, Christian understanding of the nature of being, both of God and Christ and of normative humanity, has been cast in male generic terms. This male generic understanding of being has been used to subordinate women, both as members of humanity and as persons capable of exercising authority and representing God and Christ.[17]

The sacralization of clerical power is harmful to the whole church, not only to women. Without going into an issue that would take us too far afield, it must be acknowledged that ordained men themselves fall prey to the very power bestowed upon them. Because they are members of an elite group, chosen to guard the treasures of grace, they progressively lose their own identity and sense of self. Called to image Christ, they are very often acutely aware how impossible it is to reproduce the person of Christ in their daily lives. That sense of inadequacy frequently leads to alcoholism, depression, burn-out . . . and abuse. As for the women who become the victims of their abuse, they will be told to forgive—even if the abuser never asks for forgiveness, even if he never admits to doing anything wrong—and offer up their pain in union with the passion of Christ on the altar.

This means that the men who abuse their "sacred power" are never held responsible for their actions in spite of the many inquiries made into, for instance, the manifold documented cases of sexual abuse of children.[18] To their credit, the Canadian Conference of Catholic Bishops undertook an in-depth study of this problem and published *From Pain to Hope*, which acknowledges that church leadership must be compassionate toward victims by "showing that the Church does care and will do everything possible to respond to the situation," and take responsibility "for getting to the truth of a difficult situation."[19] This attitude has yet to be applied to the cases of sexual misconduct of clergy with women or the rampant exploitation of women employed by the institutional church. There is still a widespread belief that women are either consenting partners, as in cases of sexual abuse, or power-brokers who deserve to be dismissed because they exercised far too much unofficial power. There seems to be a denial among church leaders that these abuses of power are a form of violence totally incompatible with the Gospel.

Many years ago, another group of bishops had done an extensive study on violence both in the home and in society at large. They admitted that domestic violence is rooted in a male-centered culture "supported by a whole patriarchal system of social, political, and economic and *religious* structures" that reinforce domination of men over women.[20] Clearly, unhealthy relationships between men and women, whether they take the form of wife-battering or the sexual abuse, exploitation, or harassment of women by clergy, are not about the "essential difference" in men's and women's "nature"; they are about one group insisting it has the God-given right to maintain control over the other. They are all the more abhorrent in that they are an abuse of sacred power, a breach of trust in the person whose vocation it is to teach the Word of God, lead the community in worship, and coordinate the work of bringing about the reign of God on earth.

It's important to understand how Catholic women can be misled and eventually abused or exploited by clergy because of the skewed understanding of the faith, the church, and its priesthood described earlier. But for women to begin seeing themselves as powerless victims of an authority figure in an oppressive religious system, they first have to come to recognize the imprint this system has left on their psyches. This recognition is at the very heart of their healing process. Abused women need to emerge from a posture of victims, to one of survivors of abuse, to women fully alive: in their bodies, minds, and souls.

The awareness of a systemic problem raised by women who were victims of spousal violence raises many questions about the sacred power conferred upon priests. Is the priest really the only mediator in *loco Christi* between God and the people of God? Is the Eucharist truly a sacrifice, or is it meant to be food for the spiritual journey? Is the Eucharist not more important than the gender or marital status of its presider? Given all the arguments brought forward by the magisterium to keep women outside the reach of "sacred power," does this mean that God refuses to be directly present and active in women's lives? Is God so limited? And is this the God that Jesus of Nazareth came to reveal and manifest?

As for women who have been alienated from their faith by abuse of the spiritual power of a priest, many have moved beyond the questioning phase. They have undertaken a conversion, a *metanoia* regarding their experience of God, their relationship with the sacred, and their understanding of Christian discipleship. This conversion has not been easy, but it has been, as we shall see, a source of transformation and healing.

Readings

A most accessible and helpful book for abused wives is Sheila A. Rogers, *From Fear to Freedom: Abused Wives Find Hope and Healing* (Toronto: Path Books, 2002).

For a general overview of how women are regarded and treated in the church, read Joanna Manning, *Is the Pope Catholic? A Woman Confronts Her Church* (Toronto: Malcom Lester Books, 1999), and *Take Back the Truth, Confronting Papal Power and the Religious Right* (New York: Crossroad, 2002).

There are two classics for women struggling with the issue of equality for women in the church, both written by biblical scholars: Carolyn Osiek, *Beyond Anger: On Being a Feminist in the Church* (New York/Mahwah: Paulist Press, 1986), and Sandra M. Schneiders, *Beyond Patching: Faith and Feminism in the Catholic Church* (NJ: Paulist Press, 1991 and 2004).

For the best compendium of a more comprehensive reading on the problems arising out of sexism in the church, I recommend Elisabeth Schüssler Fiorenza, ed., *The Power of Naming: A Consilium Reader in Feminist Liberation Theology* (New York: Orbis, 1996).

Notes

1. Priests are expected to be celibate and therefore the exception, but the pedophilia and sexual abuse scandal speak volumes on that issue.

2. Pope Paul VI, *Humanae Vitae—Of Human Life* (pamphlet, Pauline Books, 1968). For more on this subject, see Garry Wills, *Papal Sin* (New York: Doubleday, 2000) 89–103.

3. On this see Kathleen MacDonnell's introduction in *Side Effect: Women and the Pharmaceutical Industry* (Toronto: Women's Educational Press, 1986).

4. John Paul II, Apostolic Letter *Mulieris Dignitatem* (www.vatican.va, 15 August 1988).

5. Ibid., no. 5.

6. Ibid., no. 9.

7. Ibid., no. 10.

8. Ibid., no. 11.

9. Ibid., no. 13.

10. Ibid., no. 24.

11. Ibid., nos. 27 and 31.

12. A. W. Schaef, *When Society Becomes an Addict* (San Francisco: Harper and Row, 1987) 100.

13. Joseph Cardinal Ratzinger, "Letter to the Bishops of the Catholic Church on the Collaboration of Men and Women in the Church and in the World" (Congregation for the Doctrine of the Faith, May 31, 2004) 1.

14. Ibid., no. 2.

15. John Paul II, *Ordinatio Sacerdotalis*, Origins (Vol. 24, No. 4, June 9, 1994) no. 3.

16. Ibid., no. 4.

17. R. R. Ruether, "Women's Difference and Equal Rights in the Church," in E. Schüssler Fiorenza, ed., *The Power of Naming* (New York: Orbis, 1996) 208.

18. The sexual abuse of children by priests is probably the worst scandal to plague the Catholic Church in living memory. Many analyses have been undertaken of this tragedy, beginning with *The Report of the Archdiocesan Commission of Enquiry into the Sexual Abuse of Children by Members of the Clergy* (Archdiocese of St. John's, 1990), and more recently the U.S. Bishops' National Review Board Report (the John Jay Report, 2004).

19. Canadian Conference of Catholic Bishops, *From Pain to Hope* (Concacan, Ottawa, 1992) 22.

20. Assembly of Quebec Bishops, *A Heritage of Violence*, 27 (emphasis mine).

Chapter 5

A CHALLENGE TO THE FAITH

Women who related stories of abuse in their relationships with Catholic clergy felt that they had been robbed of their faith. Understandably, they wonder where, in this painful experience, was God? Where was Christ? Where was their faith community? Does being a Catholic really mean that women have to accept being hurt and used? Is this how women are "saved"? Is this what faith is all about? These, of course, are fundamental faith concerns of the women I interviewed. Some of them were much more vulnerable and also less educated in the faith than others. This distinction needs to be made before any attempt is made to show that the experience of abused women is consistent with a number of issues discussed by contemporary feminist theologians. A brief survey of some of the issues discussed in their works is included here for the benefit of women who feel they belong to one or the other of these groups by providing some insight into the research and critical reflection, as well as the spiritual journey, of other women in the church. It may also provide solace for those who still feel the pain of betrayal by a member of the clergy, but who are not prepared to give up, because of them, on the Catholic Church.

Women who have been sexually abused by a priest, if they still believe in God at all (many of them have not only given up on religious practice but also claim to have lost their faith altogether), want to cry out to a God of justice like the vengeful God of the Old Testament. They also find the person of Jesus somewhat frightening because a priest who is, according to church teaching, "another Christ," betrayed their trust. Once they come to understand that God is much more than any priest, greater even than the hierarchy of the church, its laws and rituals, they soon reject the idea of a God who takes satisfaction in human suffering or who can only be appeased by human sacrifice. Of those I interviewed over the past several years, few of the sexually abused women who claimed to be recovered still consider themselves Catholics. One retreat director, who works in conjunction with the Center for Sexual and Family Violence in Seattle, explained that it takes a very long time for women to recover their faith, and some never do. We both found that some women who still attend Mass or belong to a parish have not really begun their recovery process. They still show signs of being very unwell emotionally and physically, or they are still expecting church authorities to "do something" for them so they can "get over it." What exactly they expect is not clear.

Abused women certainly do not believe they have a status of human dignity on a par with men, especially priests. They have been, or still are, simply objects to be used. And because the institutional church accepts no responsibility for the harm done to them by clergy, these women have little hope of ever obtaining justice from the institution. Some of them, we know, have taken their case before the civil courts, but very often that has resulted in their being ostracized from the Christian community. The priest, his colleagues, or the bishop still have on their side the power to discredit her within the community by hinting that she is mentally deranged or lying, or that she seduced the priest. Even if they win their civil cases and get some kind of monetary settlements, it is almost always accompanied by a gag order. Attempts at restorative justice and reconciliation have not succeeded because for there to be reconciliation, there has to be forgiveness. For forgiveness to happen, there has to be a recognition of wrongdoing. This is tantamount to an admission of legal culpability in the priest's or bishop's mind that could cost the diocese large sums of money. In some dioceses in North America, bishops have begun to take responsibility for the sexual misconduct of their priests by paying for women's therapy. They have learned that these costs are nothing compared to the loss of credibility they suffer when cases of sexual misconduct are made public in the media. Still, I know of no diocese that has set up a spiritual ministry by women for women who have suffered abuse at the hands of clergy.

Such a ministry could also reach out to women who were exploited in their church work or unjustly dismissed at the whim of a bishop or pastor. The challenge to their faith is somewhat different because they firmly believed they were answering Christ's call to work in the church. They are also more likely to try to understand their faith better rather than give it up. They make a clearer distinction between God and God's ministers. When they realize they have been victims of an abuse of power, they begin to question the power structures within the church and come to the conclusion that there really is no room for women within those structures. They are then more open to exploring doctrinal viewpoints other than the essentially male ones sanctioned by the Vatican. They become more aware of the exclusively masculine language of its theology, especially through the liturgy, where God is a male Trinity of Father, Son, and Spirit, officially always referred to as "He." The exclusion of women from the altar and the pulpit quickly becomes the symbol of their invisibility within the church.

Many of these women aspire to legitimately "represent Christ" before the community; they seek a partnership in ministry based on the radical equality of men and women in the church and the recognition of all the gifts and charisms women can contribute to its service. They long for eucharistic celebrations that nurture their spiritual life and sense of belonging to a church of communion. They are disappointed with an essentially legalistic model of institutional church that refuses to change, so they tend to seek more Gospel-inspired communities that blend spirituality with concerns for social justice. When these women, who work in the church, drop from exhaustion or are summarily dismissed for an error they committed (which may or may not have been pointed out to them), they are seldom hired back. According to several who have had to leave a diocesan or parish employment, they have gone on to do other things because their colleagues seemed to consider them dangerous.

Sister Jean was one such woman. She was the director of a new evangelization project in her diocese. She asked her bishop for a six-month leave so she could take a course plus a few weeks for much-needed rest. When she left, her bishop replaced her with a woman from another religious community and told his female staff members to avoid calling her under the pretext that she needed time to rest. He privately told individual staff members that Jean was really not qualified for the important position she held, and that some of her feminist leanings were not in keeping with church doctrine. No longer employed by the diocese, Jean had to find new work elsewhere. She would have had no means of support if she pursued her studies, since she was the main wage earner in her small community; an extended leave to rebuild her health was out of the question. Even among vowed religious, there are women like Jean who eventually distance themselves from the larger institutional church that abuses them. They find support for their Catholic faith in smaller, less structured base communities that put more emphasis on social justice than on doctrine, rules, and rubrics.

Whether they are seeking a more justice-oriented faith or want to be full-fledged members of a church that has recovered its mission to spread the Good News, women who recover from an abuse of power are quite down to earth and anchored to the present. They make it their first priority to find out who they are in a world badly in need of realigning itself with the Creator's plan and to live in more harmonious and authentic human relationships. The reign of God can be found within, and the Gospel call is to share it. Perfect and unending happiness may come in another life, but crossing into it in death does not frighten them. Furthermore, they say they feel very close to the loved ones who have gone ahead, and grateful they are still present to them in some mysterious way to guide them. The most important thing in life is to live out the Gospel that gives meaning and direction to their lives, here and now. This new way of understanding the Christian faith and life finds an echo in what feminist theologians have been saying for some time now.

WOMEN EXPERIENCE CONVERSION

In the early 1980s, Rosemary Radford Ruether named the evil oppressing women in the church: sexism. In her book *Sexism and God-talk* (1983), she uses feminist methodology to approach the major themes in systematic theology: God, anthropology, christology, mariology, evil, the church, creation, and the end times. Her objective is to delineate and analyze sexist thought patterns that have led to the consecration of patriarchy within the dominant tradition, and then suggest new patterns for transformation and healing. For transformation to occur, there has to be a change of mindset; this requires personal conversion. In her chapter dealing with the awareness of evil, she describes the steps leading to conversion based on a holistic spirituality. In fact, she describes the journey of many of the women I interviewed who had never read her book.

For one thing, women learn very early on that anger and pride are cardinal mortal sins, and they should cultivate humility and self-denial, the distinctively Christian virtues. Radford Ruether notes that this should apply to all Christians, but it becomes a powerful ideology to subjugate women and deprive them of their self-esteem. Women are supposed to imitate Christ by having no "self," by becoming "suffering servants," and therefore by accepting abuse and exploitation. Conversion, then, would mean that women have to turn away from their own sin of sexism by beginning to get in touch with their anger. That is a liberating grace which would allow them to break with oppressing and sexist social structures and ideologies. Women have to recover their pride, not in the sense of looking down on others, but of acquiring a healthy self-esteem. Without it, goes on Radford Ruether, there is no self at all on which to build an identity. Women must think through for themselves and "convert" the male ideology of pride and humility.

Getting in touch with one's anger and regaining one's self-esteem are essential stages in reevaluating the unjust system in which they have been raised, a system designed to justify patriarchy and make it seem natural and willed by God. *Metanoia* or personal conversion can be a source of liberation from an alienating and skewed social conscience, one that makes victimization normal. Conversion pushes us into a new awareness that rejects ideologies which justify and support oppressive systems. It strives to create a new world based on truth and healthy relationships.

Women who succeed in recovering from an abuse of power are aware of and conversant with the sacred dwelling within them. They have experienced its divine presence and healing power. They want that experience acknowledged, in the name of the Gospel and for the sake of the truth. This is how they reclaimed their fundamental equality, in terms of their humanity, with men, even ordained men.

HUMAN NATURE AND RELATIONSHIP WITH GOD

This is the backdrop against which Anne E. Carr presents the symbolic value of women's ordination to promote a renewed Christian and Catholic understanding of humanity as created in the image and likeness of God. Carr claims there is only one human nature, shared by all women and men. Even if some functions are biologically determined, members of both sexes must develop qualities traditionally found in the other.

When I asked women to tell me about their thoughts on God and their relationship with the divine, many of their insights reflect the views of A. E. Carr. For instance, if only a male can represent Christ to the community and therefore speak authoritatively for and about God, he can only represent the male face of God. Moreover,

Women report that the official language for God, received in their churches, has given them a powerful, white, male God who is a protector, benefactor, judge, a stern but loving father who requires unquestioning obedience. It is an image of God as authoritarian, as a judge "over against" the self, humankind, the world. It is an image of God as power, in the sense of control, domination, even coercion. . . . This image of God has instilled in them a sense of their status as children, a sense of powerlessness, dependence, distrust of their own authority, experience, and knowledge. And while such perceptions may be religiously helpful correctives to men in patriarchal culture, they are no help to women in their quest for adult autonomy, interdependence, freedom, responsibility, bodily and sexual integrity and self-respect—characteristics necessary of an adult and fully Christian life. For some women this God is a terror. For others, he is irrelevant and boring."[1]

It is the right to represent Jesus Christ before the community that Anne Carr is claiming for women, since Jesus incarnates equally the human traits attributed to both men and women. Carr explains that the main objective of the prevalent teaching on the difference between men and women within the institutional church is to preserve the old order as natural, created, and revealed by God. A new anthropology is needed, based on history, experience, and the human and biological sciences. This would require the church to adopt a more progressive stance. Faith, according to Anne Carr, is both a journey and a mystery, and anthropology is more than an ideology that perpetuates the inequality between the sexes. The cultural and religious stereotypes produced by such an ideology keep women in a state of dependence upon men. The church's traditional teaching about humanity's relationship with God keeps in place a religious symbolism that reinforces patriarchal, hierarchical, political, social, and familial structures harmful to women. This religious symbolism is so profoundly entrenched in Christian theology, the structure of the church, and its liturgical practice, that its destructive and exclusive message is unconsciously internalized from birth. Only a few of the women I interviewed were familiar with the writing of Anne Carr, but their experience confirms every aspect of her theory.

UNDERSTANDING WHO CHRIST IS

Consequently, women want to be liberated from the power that oppresses them and prevents them from having access to the sacred. They begin to feel the need to name the divine mystery differently. That is precisely what Elizabeth A. Johnson does in her book *She Who Is*. She remains within "the contours of Christian faith" as she pleads for freedom from fear and ignorance in Christian living for the greater good of all creation. Her basic premise is that

> women are equally created in the image and likeness of God, equally redeemed by Christ, equally sanctified by the Holy Spirit; women are equally involved in the on-going tragedy of sin and the mystery of grace, equally called to mission in this world, equally destined for life with God in glory."[2]

She then goes on to develop her theological discourse, naming the divine Trinity differently: Spirit–Sophia (wisdom), Jesus–Sophia, and Mother–Sophia. God is not a hierarchy of persons but an incomprehensible mystery of relational communion.

Johnson goes a long way to deconstruct the Catholic Church doctrine of Christ that has so often been used to subordinate and exclude women. Because the historical Jesus was male, that maleness is considered to be the essence of God as made manifest in Christ. Consequently, following a male-centered anthropology, maleness is the norm; it is more worthy of honor, it has greater dignity because God chose to become incarnate in a male. She believes the maleness of Christ should be open to a new, more liberating interpretation for women to weave a new interdependence between men and women, setting aside the current dependence model based on the duality of the sexes.

Interdependence is the foundation of a truly evangelical life; it is realized in friendship with the poor and disenfranchised, including women, friendship that affirms human dignity and can contribute to the conversion of people who are dominated. Johnson ponders the mysteries of suffering and evil without claiming to offer answers, but she does proclaim a God who is on the side of violated and abused women, who supports all resistance to oppression and to powers that are destructive of human dignity, who calls women and men to become friends of God and prophets.

Women who have been victimized because of an exclusively sacrificial understanding of the priesthood and of the Eucharist echo Elizabeth Johnson's call for more communion-centered eucharistic celebrations that are authentic thanksgivings where Jesus, divine Wisdom, frees humanity and the world by reconciling them to God. Johnson puts words around the longing of recovering women for more significant and effective celebrations of their faith in Christ. Their search for more inclusive communities often takes them to alternative liturgies, where leadership is not dependent upon being an unmarried male. There they are encouraged to "acts of shucking off denigrating self-images, refusing victimization, blessing the body, finding one's voice and speaking the truth in all boldness."[3]

FINDING A COMMUNITY OF EQUAL DISCIPLES

Trying to find meaningful liturgies usually means looking for a different kind of church community. The desire to be treated as full-fledged members—real persons and not subjects of the clergy—seemed to be the deepest desire in the hearts of the abused church women I met. They were looking for a church where the sanctifying and healing power of the Spirit was at work, a community where they would be treated as true disciples of Jesus Christ, not second-class members. The theme of discipleship of equals is a recurrent one in the works of theologian Elizabeth Schüssler Fiorenza. In many ways, the publishing of her book *In Memory of Her: A Feminist Theological Reconstruction of Christian Origins* in 1983 was a landmark in women's history, both in the church and in society as well. First, she develops a new feminist hermeneutics and explains the process of patriarchalization of the church and theology; then she proceeds to a radical reinterpretation of the New Testament and of the first Christian communities founded on the equality of all disciples of Jesus. She then lays the foundation for a new interpretation of the kingdom of God, the *basileia* Jesus had come to establish. Her purpose is "to keep alive 'the *memoria passionis*' of Christian women" and reclaim "women's religious-theological heritage" that must be "reconstituted as a history of liberation and of religious agency." The great service she renders to the church, considering the problem abused women are dealing with, is that she names and defines the church as experienced by women, and also what an *ekklesia* of women could be.

Schüssler Fiorenza reminds us that the call to become disciples of Jesus is a call to holiness. This is particularly important for women who have been cut off from themselves and the source of holiness within themselves, and who therefore must find the sacred elsewhere than in the institutional church, its rituals, and ecclesiastical sacred power. Holiness is to be equated with human integrity: "Human holiness must express human wholeness. . . . Everydayness, therefore, can become revelatory, and the presence and power of God's sacred wholeness can be experienced in *every* human being." God's saving power is felt every time someone is healed and every time a woman who was once dismissed as worthless finds her worth in God's eyes and meaning in life. Jesus' vision of God's saving presence and activity—and therefore the mission he entrusted to his disciples—is to make people "whole, healthy, cleansed and strong. It restores people's humanity and life. This salvation . . . is not confined to the soul but spells wholeness for the total person in her/his social relations."[4] Schüssler Fiorenza also believes that it is possible to speak of God in feminine terms, since in some books of the

Old Testament, Sophia (Wisdom) is a divine figure, another face of the God of Israel. Jesus was part of that Wisdom tradition, the messenger, the prophet, the child of Sophia, the one who brings peace and healing to the world.

This is what makes the *ekklesia* of women, the work of the Spirit–Sophia, so attractive to the women who are seeking healing from clergy abuse. It involves a new community paradigm, a Christian feminist gathering of women who are empowered by the Spirit and sent forth to feed, heal, and liberate those of their own sex, particularly those who have been betrayed and broken by men entrusted with the sacred power of holy orders. This is because such a church community, according to Schüssler Fiorenza, "unmasks us and sets us free from the structural sin and alienation of sexism and propels us to become children and spokeswomen of God." It rejects the idolatrous worship of maleness and articulates the divine image in female human existence and language. It sets us free from the internalization of false altruism and self-sacrifice that is concerned with the welfare and work of men first to the detriment of our own and other women's welfare and calling. It enables us to live "for one another" and to experience the presence of God in the *ekklesia* as the gathering of women.[5]

In fact, it is this vision of a small house-church for women that inspired us as we went about the challenging task of trying to set up a support group for women who had been abused by clergy and who were struggling with the loss of faith.

Readings

Besides the books quoted in this chapter, there is a very helpful collection of essays edited by Elisabeth Schüssler Fiorenza, *The Power of Naming, a Consilium Reader in Feminist Liberation Theology* (New York: Orbis, 1996).

Notes

1. A. E. Carr, *Transforming Grace* (New York: Continuum, 1996) 140.

2. E. A. Johnson, *She Who Is: The Mystery of God in Feminist Theological Discourse* (New York: Crossroad, 1993) 8.

3. Elizabeth A. Johnson, *Friends of God and Prophets* (New York: Continuum, 1996) 231.

4. E. Schüssler Fiorenza, *In Memory of Her: A Feminist Theological Reconstruction of Christian Origins* (New York: Crossroad, 1983) 120.

5. Ibid., 346.

Chapter 6

FINDING HELP

When the director of a sexual assault clinic first invited two women to join us in setting up a support group for women who had been sexually abused by clergy, neither of them wanted to get involved. One said she was not yet over the "breakup" with the priest and was not comfortable telling her story to anyone else, especially in a group setting. The second woman was hesitant to get involved in anything so "experimental" and expressed the fear that her participation might be reported back to the priest—whom she didn't want to offend. A student doing research into methods for sexual assault intervention suggested to us that either the abused women were too ashamed to come forward for help because of what happened to them or they were still denying that they had in fact been abused. There was no point in referring these women to support groups for battered or sexually assaulted women because they did not see themselves as victims of abuse. Nor did they see themselves as codependent, so there was no point in referring them to a twelve-step program. They were not interested in any form of self-help group or group therapy where they would be expected to talk about their relationship with the priest who had hurt them. They still believed they had a duty to protect the reputation of the individual priest or bishop and the Catholic Church as a whole. Since this was also true of women who had been harassed and exploited by clergy, we came to the conclusion that they were still infatuated with the priest or the church. In a nutshell, these women did not want any help. And yet, therapists, psychiatrists, and spiritual counselors were still insisting a support group for women abused by clergy should be set up. The challenge for us was to come up with a formula these women might find attractive.

This led to consultations with women from other types of faith support groups—prayer groups, meditation groups, base communities, and Bible study groups, as well as women engaged in preventing violence against women. They and the members of their various organizations all felt a sense of being Catholic, though many of them found it difficult or even impossible to attend regular Catholic liturgies. They felt alienated by the all-male language, the exclusively male presiders, the total absence, as one woman put it, "of women in the priest's consciousness." What all these women also shared was an intense desire to still belong to the people of God, and live as full-fledged disciples of Jesus, the Christ of the Gospels. These women shared with me their own search for wholeness as female Christians. Our combined searching and reflection helped us discover the needs that had to be met in spiritually abused women and gave us some direction in finding the theological foundations for a spirituality that was both Christian and inclusive.

In reviewing the data gathered in our collective interviews and journeying with abused women, we found a number of common traits among those who said they were now "in a good space." All felt to varying degrees alienated by institutional Catholicism because of the way they had been treated, but on the other hand, they felt a deeper connection with themselves, their surroundings, and the Source of their spirituality. The women who claimed to be recovered admitted it had taken a long time to find their spiritual "center" and their self-esteem, understood as a healthy and realistic acceptance of their strengths and personal value as a human being. Most importantly, every one of them recognized that what had helped them the most was having a strong support network made up of faithful and caring friends, either among members of their religious community (a full third of the women I interviewed are or had been nuns), their family, or close acquaintances who could support them emotionally. All of them claimed to be reasonably "well"—physically, mentally, emotionally, and spiritually. They also recognized that their spirituality was the most important factor in their recovery, and that it was their relationship with their spiritual self that gave them life.

Rather than try to set up a support group for abused women, then, we decided to start a women's friendship circle for spiritual development. The diocese where I began my research had gone through the Renew process some years earlier. This is a process aimed at parish and community renewal based on small-group Scripture study. Some of the women we hoped to help knew other women who had been involved in "small-group faith sharing" or had even been involved themselves. This turned out to be a good idea, because we could also invite women to join our spirituality study group who had no recollection of ever having been abused by clergy. Consequently, the group was open to any woman who wanted to discover and explore her spirituality. It also allowed us to spread the word among counselors and therapists we knew that a new women's group existed that could be helpful for women abused by clergy. Since clergy misconduct does not happen only in the Catholic Church, the group was open to women of other faiths as well.

The main objective was exploration and discovery, so the only criterion for joining was a willingness to do the "inner work." This involves self-discovery, truth-seeking, and health-rebuilding using a holistic approach. The goal was to acquire a new Christian spirituality based on "eating together, sharing together, drinking together, talking with each other, receiving each other, experiencing God's presence through each other, and, in doing so, proclaiming the gospel as God's alternative vision for everyone, especially for those who are poor, outcast, and battered."[1]

Although it may appear exclusive, there was good reason for opening the group to women only. We were only too well aware that not only women suffer abuses at the hands of clergy, and that there is a great deal of work to do, for instance, on behalf of men who were victims of pedophiles when they were children. There are also laymen who have been dismissed without recourse from church employment after many years of service when a new pastor or bishop took over. It was simply for us a case of meeting a required need, providing a safe, sacred space for women, and respecting the requests of the people we hoped to help.

An addiction counselor gave us some helpful hints about rules to observe at the group meetings based on Al-Anon and Adult Children of Alcoholics meetings. As for group leadership and making sure our simple rules were observed during meetings, we opted for a feminist model of consensus-building and shared responsibility. Given the kind of problems we might encounter reaching out to abused women, we enlisted the help of women who had experience in group dynamics and shared leadership. We also knew that some issues were bound to be raised in time: issues of power and abuse of power, the meaning of consent in sexual relationships, acceptable work conditions, women's place in the church, and so on. It was therefore important to have someone in a leadership capacity who had sufficient training in theology, with some knowledge of the hierarchical church system, its teaching about women, and its internal workings, to respond to those issues clearly and factually. We also needed someone who had some knowledge of feminist methodology and experience of sexual assault intervention and who could respond effectively to issues involving sexual assault, exploitation, and harassment.

Having spent a great deal of time listening to the stories of women who had been abused, I knew what a wealth of experience and knowledge they could bring to our group. There is nothing quite as affirming and uplifting as hearing someone share her story and feel she is "telling my story." That would not be the obvious, prime focus of the group, however. These women would gather to share their common Christian discipleship, they would study together a given text, usually taken from Scripture, and then apply it to their own lives following a few simple rules:

1. Everything said within the group was to be considered "sacred" and therefore confidential, even though this was not "group therapy."
2. Participants would listen respectfully to one another without interrupting. There would be no right or wrong answers or interpretations to Scripture, no advice would be given, or moralizing about someone else's life. We would not have to agree with what was being said, but recognized the right of others to speak.
3. We would refrain from criticizing or blaming anyone.
4. We would speak from our own experience, not reporting someone else's.

Because our main purpose was to journey together in search of our spiritual selves and, in so doing, become a small faith community, we agreed that some important themes had to be discussed. We explained to the women that our journey together was not about climbing the ladder of spiritual success. A more appropriate image would be that of a dance where we move in and out of a "spiritual space." As Elisabeth Schüssler Fiorenza describes the steps of women's spirituality, we would opt for processes that "are not simply linear and sequential, like the steps of a staircase, rather, like steps in a dance, they move backward and forward, encircle, repeat, and move ahead once more."[2]

At all our meetings, there was a time of silent centering, a text from Scripture or other spiritual reading followed by some questions for discussion, pauses for reflection, time for expressing ourselves in prayer. Some suggestions for themes and the insights they provided are found in chapter 8. Women were encouraged to keep a journal to document their discoveries, reactions, and experience of inner growth. At the end of each meeting, we took time to break bread together, usually over a cup of tea or coffee and, occasionally, someone's favorite dessert. From our original group have sprouted several new shoots: an interfaith study group for women who meet over lunch once a month to share books and articles, discuss hot issues of the day, and discern courses of action in social justice; two small base communities of Catholic women who meet regularly for alternative liturgies and women's Eucharist; two women went on to theological schools and were ordained in other denominations; one woman completed her graduate work in theology and is now responsible for formation of the laity in a large archdiocese. We have kept in touch over the years since the first group began. All recall with gratitude that their first steps in the dance of recovery and healing, their search for spiritual and psychological "wholeness" began the day they admitted to themselves that they had been victims of some kind of abuse of power by a member of the clergy.

Readings

An excellent source of inspiration, particularly for women who are searching for alternative sources for prayer and meditation, is H. Ward, J. Wild, and J. Morley, *Celebrating Women* (Harrisburg, PA: Morehouse Publishing, 1995). Also very helpful is Dorothea McEwan, Pat Pinsent, Ianthe Pratt, and Veronica Seddon, *MAKING LITURGY: Creating Rituals for Worship and Life* (Norwich: Canterbury Press, 2001).

Notes

1. Elisabeth Schüssler Fiorenza, *In Memory of Her: A Feminist Theological Reconstruction of Christian Origins* (New York: Crossroad, 1983) 348.

2. Elisabeth Schüssler Fiorenza, *But SHE Said: Feminist Practices of Biblical Interpretations* (Boston: Beacon Press, 1992) 9.

Chapter 7

CONFRONTING SPIRITUAL ABUSE

Many devout and dedicated Catholic women, as I said at the beginning, find it extremely difficult to tackle a problem in the church such as an abuse of power. They are afraid of losing their faith or of being misunderstood or even ostracized from their faith community. This indicates how important their faith is in their lives, and how loyal they still want to be to an institution they believe to be holy in spite of the failings of its ministers. Because of these conflicting emotions, it takes considerable courage for women who have been sexually abused by their priest or who have been exploited or dismissed from their church work for no justifiable reason to even begin the process of recovery. Those who achieve some measure of well-being, of wholeness, acknowledge that they are involved in a work in progress. They have altered many beliefs, behaviors, and attitudes that made them codependent regarding clergy and their "sacred power." Many have also had to put some distance, at least for a time, between themselves and the institutional church. A considerable number leave the church altogether.

As with any other form of recovery or healing journey, the search for spiritual and psychological wholeness begins with awareness. Many of the women I interviewed were still struggling with such things as serious health problems, shaky personal relationships, or financial difficulties due to lack of employment, but they knew one thing: they would have to change to find healing and meaning in their lives. So they were determined to "do whatever it takes" to achieve their goal. They usually began by seeking some kind of spiritual help, most often from another priest. This seldom seemed to work, perhaps because of the unconscious association in their minds with the priest who abused them. Whatever the reason, those who arrived at some measure of physical, psychological, and spiritual well-being attribute it to the understanding, support, and nurturing of other women who guided them into a new spirituality—one that met the needs of their entire person: body, mind, and soul. Then, and this is a crucial common trait, recovering women gave themselves permission to question their beliefs about the power that the priest had over them, and how this had affected their understanding of God, Jesus Christ, the church, and the meaning of life. To do this they were supported by women who understood the dynamic of abuse, could explain religious concepts in terms they understood, and showed a willingness to share their own spiritual experiences. Also, they were prepared to search for answers with them rather than provide ready-made ones.

As recovering women begin to look at their relationships with themselves and with others, they come to realize that they had fallen into the trap of living for the approval of others. They also acknowledge their lack of self-esteem and personal boundaries, their tendency to be controllers, to feel everybody else's feelings for them, and the fact that they have betrayed some of their most fundamental and deep-seated moral principles. There is also a profound sense of frustration and anger that they have been denied access to the sacred. They are confused about what is truly sacred, what holiness really means, but they sense that if they want to lead a holy life, it will mean learning all over again what being a disciple of Jesus Christ is all about. This, in turn, leads them to a completely different understanding of their faith and its place in their lives.

SEARCHING FOR ONE'S "SACRED SPACE"

Journeying inward, these women began the search for their "self," their center, the inner space where they discover the essence of who they are. That is where they come into the presence of the sacred, a divine presence and activity that makes them feel loved, valued, and fully alive. A friend of mine who had worked for eighteen years as a diocesan pastoral services coordinator was dismissed without notice when she asked for a leave of absence to deal with a number of health concerns. She describes how she felt after many years of trying to recover from such an abuse of power:

> I was totally broken. It took years for me to find out who I am deep inside—and where to find God. I always thought God was "out there" some place. One day, I was reading the Bible and it hit me: if I asked God's Spirit to heal me, I was inviting God into my life. And, as I read Luke 10:10, where it says that God answers prayers and gives the Spirit to those who ask, I realized God is IN me. This moment turned my life around, it actually gave me a whole new life. I finally became comfortable with who I am because of the conviction that God loves me just as I am. But also, I am also more honest with myself about my strengths and weaknesses. I'm happier and much more energetic. I've also rediscovered how creative I can be, I've regained my self-confidence and actually find joy inside.

There is also a new imaging and naming of God as less male and patriarchal. This same woman spoke of God as Presence, Wisdom, Divine Other. As for many other women searching for God, the Holy Spirit takes on a more important role in their lives.

Marion was sexually assaulted by a retreat director when she was a novice in a religious community. This eventually led her to leave the community because her superiors did not believe her story, but insisted instead that she get psychiatric help. In therapy, she did get help to begin healing the wounds of sexual abuse. For years she wanted nothing to do with church, religion, or prayer. In time she came to understand that not only had she been physically violated, she had been robbed of her very soul. She told me:

I had been hurt by men who thought they were God. When I eventually started to pray again, I went searching inward for a feminine presence. For a long time, I thought I was praying to Our Lady, but when I began reading Wisdom Scriptures, I realized that God was both female and male. I began to feel God's Spirit as a female presence surrounding me.

When I asked recovering women what place Christ occupies in their lives, most were very taken with the Jesus they find in the Gospels, particularly in his conversations and interactions with women. This validated their personal experience of connection with Jesus, of being called to discipleship and mission, and the indwelling of the Spirit, whether or not the experience had been validated or approved by the church's priest. In a word, they had discovered that the sacred is not something "out there" from which they are excluded, or a reality reserved for "some people," but it is where they find God. One spiritual director sums up the inner spiritual dynamic of women who have found the sacred:

> What is sacred for these women, is being well—at every level of their being. They find God in all things, but especially in their deepest selves. That God, called Thou, Spirit, Presence, Divine Love, teaches them to take care of themselves, to accept themselves as gifted by God, to love themselves.

RESTORING PERSONAL BOUNDARIES

The lack of personal boundaries dates back, according to all the women I interviewed, to an incident from their childhood where they felt completely helpless with someone who had some kind of power over them. Their person, either their body, their self-esteem, or their talents had been appropriated by someone through violence, humiliation, or shame. As adults, they have had to make a conscious decision to take back their own power by establishing their own boundaries. They have had to learn to speak for themselves, defend their opinions, insist that others respect their personal space, and affirm themselves when they knew they were right. Instead of always trying to please others, they now take responsibility for their own needs and wants, especially to protect themselves from those who would harm them. Because so many of them had been victims of child sexual abuse or violence, they have learned to recognize the evil of abuse, call it by name, and never again tolerate sexual assault, exploitation, or harassment.

Their whole person has become a sacred reality, an inviolable dwelling place for the divine. They refuse to be inappropriately ashamed—that feeling of always being responsible when something goes wrong, not being good enough, being fundamentally unworthy and inferior—and know the difference between guilt and responsibility. Amy lost her husband to cancer and her only son to a car accident within a period of six months. Her pastor began to visit her on a regular basis and initiated a sexual relationship that lasted several years. When Amy wanted to end the relationship because she believed it was morally wrong, her pastor claimed it was in God's plan for them, and besides, he was simply doing his pastoral duty by "meeting her natural needs for companionship and sex." This made her feel even more guilty and ashamed. She wrote,

> I was ashamed because I didn't refuse to have sex with the priest, even though I knew it was wrong. I thought it was my fault and that I should have said no. Now I realize how vulnerable I was, and that he was the one who took advantage of me. He is the guilty one. Now I am responsible to not let this happen again.

Women recovering from abuse of power also learn to make a distinction between the Gospel imperative to help others and the manipulative call to excessive dedication. This meant, for some committed Christian women, that they could say no to tasks that were not in their job description, such as writing the pastor's homily, training laypeople on weekends, leading sacramental preparation sessions on their evening off, and so on, without feeling guilty. One respondent explained that unpaid work is the most common way of crossing women's boundaries because it is a way of appropriating women's time and talents, and deciding for them how they will respond to God's call to serve. On the other hand, these same women learn to respect the "self" of others by avoiding second-guessing their needs or pretending to know what they think and want.

REBUILDING SELF-ESTEEM

For the woman who is attempting to rebuild her life after an abuse of power, regaining self-esteem involves recognizing that she has indeed been abused, and her boundaries have been crossed, but she does have personal value and dignity from "being priceless in God's eyes," created in God's image. Personal worth does not stem from the opinion that others may have of her, nor from the approval of a clergy member. Her life has value in and of itself; being becomes more important than doing. So, she also tends to be less of a perfectionist. The Gospel call to "be perfect" is understood as the human quest to be more truly herself and lead a more balanced life. Holiness begins with a wholesome humanity. Love of self is colored and enriched by tolerance for self and others, and a good dose of humor. Louise, who had done volunteer sacramental preparation in her parish for years, was fired when she applied for the pastoral assistant's position. For a long time she thought that, in spite of her brilliant qualifications, it was because she just wasn't good enough. Now, while she can recognize her gifts and talents, she need not measure her worth solely on her performance. She wrote in her journal,

> I know when I've done my best. I know my limitations, and the fact that everyone else has theirs too. I don't compare myself to others nearly as much, and find I'm less envious of others. I can admit my mistakes, but I can also handle praise. I tend to be much more forgiving, too.

Self-esteem begins by paying attention to one's own feelings. These women will say that the Spirit speaks to them through their emotions, that feelings such as extreme neediness are neither good nor bad, but have to be acknowledged. One woman spoke of a "helpless God," meaning one who suffered with her, and who transformed her pain into serenity and eventually into joy. That inner joy was characteristic of many recovering women I met. More than one quoted Galatians 2:22 ("The fruits of the Spirit are love, joy, peace . . .").

As they recover their self-esteem, they let go of many "old absolutes," the name they give to the infallible and untouchable teachings they no longer subscribe to. Many claim to be grateful for having been raised in the Catholic faith, because it allowed them to discover the person and teaching of Jesus, but they feel alienated in an institution that uses exclusively male language and where "sacred power" is still used to oppress women and keep them in a state of submission. They find it very difficult to cultivate self-esteem when the church is constantly reminding them that they are "defective" or at best, second-class citizens.

THE ABILITY TO "LIVE AND LET LIVE"

Recovering church women attach a great deal of importance to their personal dignity, their freedom, and their right to find happiness. As they take responsibility for their own personal growth and development, they become truly mature and autonomous adults. They no longer feel they are to blame for the behavior of others, in particular the priests who abused them (that is their responsibility), nor do they feel they carry the weight of the whole church on their shoulders. They also realize that they have no control over what happens within the institutional church, so they "let go" of the idea of trying to "change them" (the members of the hierarchy).

Taking care of their own well-being does not prevent them from seeing the harm that was done to them and the injustices still being done to others. Gradually, they see the importance of solidarity with other victims, and as recovering women heal, they find the strength to denounce these injustices and share with other women their experience of abuse—and of recovery. All the women who left the church said how difficult it was to detach from the institution and its teachings that they found irretrievably sexist. Many still hoped they would someday find a faith community where they would feel welcome and equal, where their spiritual journey would be honored as well as their aspirations to live as truly *Christian* women.

AWARENESS OF THE PAIN OF OTHERS

Many of the women who told me their story first appeared to be very self-centered, virtually uncaring about other victims, and quite manipulative. This was particularly the case with women who had been sexually abused. However, as they progressed with their healing—which sometimes did not begin in earnest until the relationship had been over for many years—they wanted to get well and then help other women. The story of Ellen is telling in this regard:

> When I was in my teens, our youth group had a leader who was very controlling and emotionally abusive. He insisted on seeing me on a regular basis for spiritual direction (I wanted to become a nun), and this eventually led to various forms of sexual improprieties, which today are considered sexual assault. I tried to tell my pastor once about Father X, because I knew that the sex part had to be terribly wrong, but he would not hear the details, implied that I was lying, and told me to keep this to myself because Father X was a saintly man. I moved away from the parish and did not begin to deal with the abuse until many years later, when I landed in the hospital with severe depression. My therapist was the one who validated my story of abuse. She suggested I contact a nun who might be able to help me. Together we tracked down six other women who had been abused by the same priest! We shared our stories—essentially all the same—and eventually found the courage to report the priest to his bishop (who told us the priest was no longer involved in spiritual direction). Now, at least, we have each other's friendship and

support to rebuild our lives, and we volunteer at the local sexual assault center on a regular basis.

Many victims manage to convert their own pain and anger into energy for preventing others from having to suffer the same way. Having experienced being treated as an object to be used and abused, they know personally how victims feel and can reach out to them. They are particularly adept at helping them overcome their fears or at least putting them into perspective. One of their own greatest fears was that there would be reprisals—not the least of which was excommunication for "spreading ugly lies about the clergy" and eternal damnation "for attacking God in the person of the priest"—if they spoke to anyone about the abuse. When they do break the silence, having found the courage to speak the truth, it is to seek justice not only for themselves but also for others. Helping others is an important aspect of healing. A sexual assault counselor described recovering victims in these terms:

> When these women have been working at the healing process for a while, they learn to become less manipulative, and can be genuinely helpful with other victims. They can be very generous of their time, though they still struggle for patience and tact and must resist the urge to try to fix everybody! They have dedicated a lot of time to their own recovery . . . but once they begin to "get better," they develop a wonderful sense of humor, can laugh more easily and heartily, which is contagious. I'm sure it's because they are much more comfortable with themselves.

RECOVERING MORAL CONSCIENCE

Women who need to grieve the loss of their sense of what is morally right or wrong through abuse of religious power seek moral anchors in new forms of spirituality. Those who choose to remain in the church or to call themselves Christians find guidance in the Scriptures that they read, pray, and share with others. They explore the many facets of the life of Jesus and search in earnest for truth in his teaching. Jesus becomes the enemy of all lies, and consequently, being a disciple requires greater honesty with oneself and with others. One married woman, who eventually had to resign as parish youth coordinator because she wanted to end her sexual involvement with her pastor, confessed,

> Having been told by a priest that what I was doing was right, when I knew it was wrong, left me in a state of moral confusion. I realized I had learned to justify and rationalize immoral behavior, things that were not right. Now, I question my actions and motives, I ask myself who I am trying to please or impress, and above all, I ask myself if what I am doing is harmful to myself or others, or bottom line, if this is what Jesus would do. It's not easy being that honest—it means making some tough choices. Jesus made some very tough choices. He paid dearly, too.

It is this search for truth and honesty that helps abused women regain their sense of right and wrong. They also discover that they were misled, and understand better how they could have "accepted" being abused. This inner work requires that they revisit their family history—most often dysfunctional—where they originally learned the values promoted by a patriarchal and sexist church, where "Father" was always right. Many, if not all, of the women I interviewed had to deal with unhealed wounds dating back to childhood sexual abuse, incest, and physical or emotional violence. Often, they too first sought the help of another priest. This is understandable when we appreciate to what degree clerical power is sacralized, because the priest is God's representative, the one person she should be able to trust. Initially, for vulnerable women who have been victims of childhood sexual abuse, the priest showed them a degree of kindness they had not experienced with the men in their lives—be it father, brother, or spouse. They were somewhat overwhelmed by the goodness, love, and gentleness they saw in the priest. Every woman said: "I really trusted that man" who eventually abused her. They must therefore examine very carefully their relationship with all priests. One counselor explains the dilemma this way:

Let's not forget that the priest can be very attractive and appealing by the very fact that he has all this spiritual power. We have been taught that they embody for us the love of God, the person of Christ. So, at first, the woman cannot see herself as victim of abuse. She is totally bereft of self-esteem and internal authority at that point. Her whole life has been centered on pleasing the priest and meeting his approval. She has to work very hard to face the real feelings she has for this man who turns out to be a predator and a user, and the fact that she must give him up because the relationship is destroying her. It boils down to giving up dependence on him emotionally and spiritually, having to learn to live her life "from the inside" without constantly waiting for a man to take care of her emotionally or tell her what to do. But this is the only way she will stop being a victim.

Giving up being a victim is an important step on the road to conversion. This means not letting themselves be re-victimized, remain passive in the face of abuse, or fail to demand that their bodily integrity, as well as their emotional and spiritual integrity, be respected. What is also wrong is for them to keep silent in the face of injustice and to do nothing to prevent it from happening again.

Conversion, however, can be a long and arduous process. It is the hope of being free of shame and fear, of no longer feeling misunderstood and isolated, which allows them to foresee a new and better life. This may explain the spiritual flexibility they acquire, once they have taken ownership of what happened to them, and their openness to new ways of understanding God, Jesus, the church, morality, and the meaning of life. One spiritual director understands the conversion of women abused by clergy as

having the right to question everything, especially those "old tapes," the so-called truths inculcated in them as children that do not correspond to their experience as adult women. They no longer accept the male (church) institution's ready-made answers. They ask the vital questions, the most frequent one being, "Is this what Jesus came to teach us?"

THE CONVERSION PROCESS

All the women who shared with me their experience of abuse of power—be it sexual assault, unjustified dismissal, or accepting to stay in a violent marriage—say their decision to change their lives was triggered by an event that abruptly put an end to their denial. This is borne out by the findings of therapists and counselors. For those who were sexually abused, it was most often the discovery that the priest had another "lover," which the priests admitted, or when he was transferred out of the parish and ordered to stay away from her by his bishop. The women themselves seldom put an end to the relationship. Even when they are told that they are showing all the signs of being abused or battered, they deny it. As long as the priest is in the woman's life, she will not even consider that she could be a victim of abuse or even codependent. She believes that she and the priest are in love, and others "just don't understand."

The situation is similar with women who have been victims of extreme cases of sexual exploitation and unjustified dismissal. They feel it was all a misunderstanding, not a case of deliberate abuse of power. They tend to forgive immediately, because, after all, Jesus forgave and the Gospels command us to do the same. When they end up in a doctor's office, burned out, depressed, or even suicidal, they do not initially attribute any of this to the fact that they have been treated unfairly. Very often, these women are reluctant to avail themselves of any kind of therapy or psychological help, especially if it means consulting someone who may not share their religious beliefs. They seem to be afraid that those beliefs will be questioned or put in doubt, that they will have to examine closely, and judge, the priest's behavior and their own, as well as the teachings of the church. They also hesitate to get involved in any spiritual process not in line with established institutional church practices.

All the women I spoke to said they felt the need to be forgiven for the sins they had committed, even if the sin was hard to identify. So they would begin by intensifying their religious devotions—daily Mass, prayer services, sacramental confession, and fasting—but never feeling any better. Some were even further victimized, made to assume all the guilt, or condemned outright. One woman was told in the confessional that the cancer she had developed was not punishment enough for the damage she had caused the church by accusing a priest of not treating his employees according to the social doctrine of the church! Another was told by a diocesan official to whom she complained that it was no wonder her pastor had fired her—she had far too much power in that parish anyway. And so the women come to believe that God, speaking through various church ministers, has not really forgiven them. For a time they do not know where to go to find spiritual comfort and inner peace. They feel more guilt than ever. It is only when they get professional counseling that they can get to the bottom of their guilt feelings and discover that they are not solely responsible for what went wrong. With spiritual support, they discover a God who is truly forgiving; they take ownership of what they have done wrong—such as allowing the injustice to go on—and resolve to change and make amends where needed. This "inner work" is what empowers them to begin healing.

All the women I interviewed told me how important it was to have found women to journey with them as they did their inner work, because they felt understood rather than blamed. The few women who received support from another priest said it was he who suggested they find a woman spiritual advisor or a good lay therapist. One important element was that their counselors convinced them it was important to take care of their physical health. That was the only way to build up enough spiritual and emotional stamina to face what they were going to find deep inside themselves.

THE IMPORTANCE OF BEING HEARD

The decision to get on with their lives is closely connected to first having their story heard and believed. It was essential that their pain finally be taken seriously and that they were not judged. One woman had a nervous breakdown when she was told she had to give up her job as parish secretary on the grounds that she was unsuitable for the position, since she and the new pastor had "conflicting personalities." Yet she had never once been reprimanded by him. She wrote in her response to my questionnaire:

> I couldn't understand why I was so depressed over losing my job. I was being treated for attempted suicide. I mentioned to the psychiatrist that I had had a sexual relationship with a priest when I was a young woman, but that was a long time ago and I had put all that behind me when I got married. He told me, at the end of one session, that he knew a social worker who was a "good Catholic" and that maybe if I could put some of my religious concerns to her (he was an atheist), she might understand "this kind of thing." I told her all about my relationship with that priest. Never did she make me feel like a tramp or a liar. . . . She also helped me question if perhaps my desire to work for the church was really a need I felt to atone for the sin of the priest who had raped me.

Other respondents maintain that it was the openness and the nonjudgmental attitude that made them suspect that they may not have been the only guilty ones in what had happened with the priest. The fact that they could express out loud the guilt they harbored, and the solidarity they felt in meeting women who had been through the same thing they had (or knew someone who had), helped validate their experience. This recognition of their experience allowed the abused women to face up to a painful reality: they had lost something very precious and that loss had created a great void in their lives. To fill that void, they first had to grieve their loss.

TAKING TIME TO GRIEVE

Whether it was the presence in her life of a man she thought was in love with her or the satisfaction of accomplishing rewarding work in the church, the magnitude of the loss these women have sustained is only understood when they begin to talk about it. Every one of them, in retrospect, admits to having had to live through various phases of grief. Here is how Amy describes this aspect of her journey:

> One evening, I arrived at the rectory unannounced, really needing to talk to my pastor. A woman I knew from the parish answered the door. I was shocked, and rumors I had heard that I was not the only woman in this man's life immediately came to mind. I asked him for an explanation. He said, "For heaven's sake, go home. Call me tomorrow." I couldn't believe what was really happening, so the next day I called and apologized for my behavior. When he said we should stop seeing one another, I got angry at him for betraying my trust, and said I would call the bishop. The bishop wouldn't see me but referred me to one of his assistants, a priest. This man told me to have my lawyer call their lawyer if I wanted to press charges, but to seriously consider the damage that would do to the church, to say nothing of the money it would cost, and after all, he said, "Father is a good priest." He then told me the best thing I could do was forgive and forget and move on. I never understood how I could forgive someone who never admitted he hurt me, that what he did was wrong, so I decided for my own sanity that I had to move on. It was a long struggle, and in my pain all I could do was pray that God would help me see clearly where my relationship with my pastor was going. I eventually came to accept that he never did really love me.

As they progressed through the stages of grief to find self-acceptance and inner peace, many women prayed for help from above. They prayed to be healed, but often did not even know where to begin finding the God who was supposed to be able to help them. It should also be mentioned that they had to grieve their loss of a church that made them feel extremely alienated, not to mention the church ministers who had sorely disappointed or even betrayed them. This is what prompted the need to search out and explore new avenues of spirituality.

All the women I spoke with confided that their recovery hinged on having learned to pray in a different way. Because they wanted to maintain their Christian faith, they first tried to explore different methods of prayer, such as praying silently. Some joined Christian meditation groups, others received help from a "prayer partner" or a spiritual mentor. Still others simply found the help they needed in books on silent prayer. They all mentioned "learning to be silent." All of these women prayed, every day. A few of them had formal theological and spiritual training; all attended church regularly; some had a great devotion to Mary and recited their rosary each day, while others focused on reading and meditating on passages from Scripture. The women who had come along furthest in their recovery admitted that, in fact, they had never learned to practice real interior silence at all. One woman who humorously described herself as a "churchaholic" said she "said a lot of prayers" but did not take time to "listen in silence," because all she would hear was an inner "scolding" from God the Father, whom she saw as distant and demanding, much like her own father.

Learning to be comfortable with silence comes only in stages, because it can be quite difficult for the grieving woman to fill the space of her aloneness. She can't find God until she comes to terms with who she is—a person loved by God. The dynamics of silence require some effort, but in the end can be extremely helpful. Here is how one spiritual guide describes the process:

> To find silence, we must learn to breathe. It is in following our breath that we begin to journey inward and become aware of what is "going on inside." That is where abused women discover the intense anger they are carrying inside, and which is at the root, I believe, of their depression. Touching their anger enables women to come out of denial and speak the secrets they have been keeping and which are making them ill. If they can share

these secrets, in their intimate detail, with someone they trust, they can relive all the emotional trauma they experienced, acknowledge what was done to them, recognize that this was wrong and they are not responsible. They realize they had no control over those events but can take some control over their lives now. They empower themselves to heal.

There are exercises that can help a person learn to breathe. "Silence and breathing," said one woman respondent, "helped me listen to the needs of my body. Little by little, I became aware that my whole body needed caring. I was extremely tired and had all kinds of health problems. I believe that the silence at the end of each breath opened up a way to reach healing, one breath at a time, for my body, my feelings, and my soul."

On the subject of anger, psychotherapist Lois Frankel also believes that at the root of much depression in women is an anger turned inward.[1] The anger comes from not having any control over their personhood, their life, their relationships with others within the family or the couple, or in the work world. Once women recognize that anger can be transformed into positive energy, they begin to take ownership of their lives. They experience a newfound inner freedom that enables them to develop a whole new spiritual life.

Readings

There are many books that deal with the grieving process. Several women recommended Jean Monbourquette, *How to Forgive* (Montreal: Novalis, 1992). They found it very helpful, since it deals with different types of loss (death, divorce, separation, and so on). For those who need help in praying through this difficult process, I recommend Joyce Rupp, o.s.m., *Praying Our Goodbyes* (Notre Dame, IN: Ave Maria Press) 1990.

Notes

1. Lois P. Frankel, *Women, Anger and Depression: Strategies for Self-Empowerment* (Deerfield Beach, FL: Health Communications Inc., 1992) 75.

Chapter 8

SPIRITUAL PATHWAYS TO RECOVERY

The next few pages contain some of the Scripture[1] passages that have served as a springboard for meditation and discussion to help women move forward in their spiritual journey. Also included are some of the discoveries and insights of the participants who experienced the sacred and the holy in new and different ways. They shared them in the hope that those who read this book may find them helpful. There is no particular order to follow in using these suggestions for meditation and prayer because each journey is different, and some themes may need more time for pondering than others.

FINDING OUR VALUE IN GOD'S EYES

For it was you who formed
    my inward parts;
You knit me together in my
    mother's womb.
I praise you, for I am
    fearfully and wonderfully made.
Wonderful are your works;
    that I know very well.
          —*Psalm* 139:13-14

Do not fear, for I have
    redeemed you;
I have called you by name,
    you are mine.
Because you are precious in
    my sight,

and honored, and I love

you . . .

—Isaiah 43:1, 4

Part of recovering our self-esteem involves accepting God's invitation to be true to ourselves and finding what gives us our human dignity. Some women at this point like to list the qualities they like about themselves and give thanks to the Source of all gifts. They also acknowledge that it is now their responsibility to cultivate these gifts in a spirit of thanksgiving.

SEARCHING FOR GOD'S PRESENCE WITHIN

For what human being knows what is truly human except the human spirit that is within? So also no one comprehends what is truly God's except the Spirit of God. Now we have received not the spirit of the world, but the Spirit that is from God, so that we may understand the gifts bestowed on us by God. . . . Do you not know that you are God's temple and that God's Spirit dwells in you? . . . God's temple is holy, and you are that temple.

—1 Corinthians 2:11-12; 3:16-17

Part of the difficulty in learning to be silent and present to oneself is the fear of not finding one's own "sacred space" where God dwells. One woman said that as she read this passage, she found herself "begging God" for an increase of faith and trust that God was speaking to her through these words. She goes on to explain:

Eventually, it dawned on me that I had to take that "leap of faith" and believe that I had indeed received the Spirit of God when I was baptized. I hadn't thought about that for years. When I resolved to believe, a peace came over me so moving that I started to cry. I think allowing those tears to flow was the starting point of my healing journey. My very soul had been violated, and I needed to cry . . .

LIVING IN EXILE AND LEAVING THE PAST BEHIND

Exile and desert wandering are familiar biblical themes that resonate in the hearts of women who feel alienated and excluded from the official faith community. Living in exile, having to leave good things behind, brings with it a sense of grief and loss. As the pain wells up, tears can be truly sacramental, a source of God's grace in a time of abandonment. In being compassionate with ourselves and with others, we receive the grace to eventually forgive and even seek reconciliation.

> But I call upon God,
>   and the LORD will save me.
> Evening and morning and at
>   noon
>   I utter my complaint and
>   moan,
>   and he will hear my voice.
> He will redeem me
>   unharmed
> from the battle that I wage,
>   for many are arrayed
>   against me.
>   —Psalm 55:16-18

The story of Hagar in Genesis 16 is particularly meaningful to women who have been used and then rejected by someone they loved and respected. Many beautiful prayers too numerous to include here sprang spontaneously from women who identify with Hagar and the injustices she suffered. A sense of human solidarity develops that gives women the courage and support they need to move on with their lives.

FINDING A WOMAN'S SPIRITUALITY

Some Gospel stories, such as the Samaritan woman in John 4 and the woman taken in adultery in John 8, are particularly useful in helping women discover a spirituality based on an intimate relationship with Christ. It is their friendship with Christ that gives them a greater sense of their worth and human dignity. This in turn prompts women to explore how they are called to live out the Christian message and what specific task Christ calls them to. The following text was helpful to many in discovering their own special giftedness:

> . . . so we, who are many, are one body in Christ, and individually we are members one of another. We have gifts that differ according to the grace given to us: prophecy, in proportion to faith; ministry, in ministering; the teacher, in teaching; the exhorter, in exhortation; the giver, in generosity; the leader, in diligence; the compassionate, in cheerfulness.
>
> Let love be genuine; hate what is evil, hold fast to what is good; love one another with mutual affection; outdo one another in showing honor. Do not lag in zeal, be ardent in spirit, serve the Lord. —*Romans 12:5-11*

SEEKING TOGETHER THE FACE OF GOD

Because traditional church language portrays God as male (Father–Son–Spirit referred to as "He"), new and meaningful ways need to be explored to help women describe or even name the divine. The most classic example is the description of the feminine face of God in Wisdom Scriptures. As Christians, women come to see Jesus Christ as the incarnation of Sophia–Wisdom:

> Wisdom is radiant and unfading,
> and she is easily discerned by those who love her,
> and is found by those who seek her.
> She hastens to make herself known to those who desire her.
> One who rises early to seek her will have no difficulty,
> for she will be found sitting at the gate.
> To fix one's thought on her is perfect understanding,
> and one who is vigilant on her account will soon be free of care,
> because she goes about seeking those worthy of her,
> and she graciously appears to them in their paths,
> and meets them in every thought.
> —*Wisdom 6:12-17*

Searching for the face of God leads to finding divine presence and activity in others as well as self, be it a loving spouse, an understanding friend, a newborn child, the grateful smile of people we are called to care for.

DEVELOPING NEW RITUALS

A new spirituality and prayer life calls for new rituals to express them. New meaning can be given to older, more traditional rites, such as breaking bread and raising a glass of wine before an ordinary meal that then takes on a eucharistic quality.

> They devoted themselves to the apostles' teaching and fellowship, to the breaking of bread and the prayers. . . . [T]hey broke bread at home and ate their food with glad and generous hearts, praising God and having the goodwill of all the people.
> —*Acts* 2:42, 46-47

Prayer, fasting, forgiveness, and reconciliation take on a new significance. Particular emphasis is put on avoiding what is sometimes called "cheap grace"—the premature forgiving of a person who has hurt you when there has been no indication of repentance for the harm done. Lengthy discussion often takes place around the issue of forgiving, based on this text from Luke:

> If another disciple sins, you must rebuke the offender, and if there is repentance, you must forgive. And if the same person sins against you seven times a day, and turns back to you seven times and says, "I repent," you must forgive.   —*Luke* 17:3-4

Many women struggle with forgiveness, precisely because there has been no repentance, no apology, no recognition of wrong-doing by the offending priest, no attempt at true reconciliation. This could explain why women, especially in sexual abuse cases, take so long to recover. The issue of forgiveness has perhaps best been expressed by Yvonne Maes, herself a victim of sexual abuse by her retreat director, a priest:

> Forgiveness is a big issue for most Christians. I've noticed that it is the weak who are asked to forgive the strong over and over again. Jesus talked about a brother forgiving a brother, not a son

> forgiving his father. Forgiveness is between equals. If the Church counsels forgiveness, then the Church has but one choice: strip the priest abuser of ordination—then and only then is there a possibility that the victim can be equal to the offender. After restitution is made, the victim could choose to forgive—any other scenario is further coercion of the victim so the offender can feel good.[2]

Women who have been dismissed unfairly try to find ways of being church outside the institution for much the same reason: the wrong done to them was never acknowledged; consequently, no apology ever made. Yet, they too are told to forgive and move on with their life. Before one pastoral assistant could forgive her pastor, she had to learn to forgive herself:

> I always felt it was my own fault that my pastor had me dismissed, even though he never told me why he didn't want me working in the parish anymore. One day, a small group of women invited me to their Bible study and prayer group. They told me what a good job I had been doing for the parish. This helped me regain some confidence in my abilities, but what struck me was that they said, at one point: "We are the church too, you know, and we find nothing wrong in what you did. Let go of the guilt. It's not yours in the first place."

LETTING THE SPIRIT TRANSFORM LIVES

Earlier we considered the process of conversion. For abused women, that often means learning to love again, starting with ourselves, establishing our boundaries and understanding we are no longer victims because we have learned to say no to oppression.

> [O]ne of the police standing nearby struck Jesus on the face, saying, "Is that how you answer the high priest?" Jesus answered, "If I have spoken wrongly, testify to the wrong. But if I have spoken rightly, why do you strike me?"   —John 18:22-23

One woman relates her understanding of this passage from John:

I was so used to imagining Jesus as this gentle and passive person who never got angry and went to his death without protesting. I meditated on this passage for a long time because I could imagine Jesus standing up to the man who was hitting him, telling him to stop. It gave me the courage to face the priest who abused me and say: "What you did was wrong. Because of what you did to me, I am no longer a Catholic, I am not even sure God exists." Oddly enough, after I said that to him, it occurred to me that he (the priest) was neither God, nor the church, so he could go to hell as far as I was concerned. I felt God and Christ were on my side, honoring my righteous anger.

ALLOWING HEALING TO HAPPEN

Recognizing the abuse of power and breaking the silence surrounding it comes more easily when women read the strong language Jesus uses to denounce the abuse of religious power in Matthew 23. Other passages can give them hope for healing at every level of their being.

> Thus says the Lord GOD to these bones: I will cause breath to enter you, and you shall live. I will lay sinews on you, and will cause flesh to come upon you, and cover you with skin, and put breath in you, and you shall live . . .   —*Ezekiel 37:5-6*

LETTING GO OF FEAR

One of the greatest fears expressed by women recovering from abuse of any kind is that of displeasing others and being rejected, diminished, or humiliated as a consequence. They also fear being judged and punished for breaking rules that are, essentially, man-made.

> But now we are discharged from the law, dead to that which held us captive, so that we are slaves not under the old written code but in the new life of the Spirit.   —*Romans 7:6*

> There is no fear in love, but perfect love casts out fear; for fear has to do with punishment, and whoever fears has not reached perfection in love.   —*1 John 4:18*

Women feel the need to question what they call old absolute rules with a broader Christian faith based on a closer reading of Scriptures such as these. They feel the need to replace inadequate ecclesiastical rulings developed in a patriarchal context and find new role models among their spiritual mothers such as women saints, mystics, and other women who have inspired them. In building smaller faith communities, they discover ways to take concrete measures to help others who have been abused or wounded. This is the way they live out the Gospel message, the way they "are church." Instead of trying to please and appease others, they work for authentic justice, in defense of others' most basic human rights.

> I am the LORD, I have called
>   you in righteousness,
>   I have taken you by the
>   hand and kept you;
> I have given you as a
>   covenant to the
>   people,
>   a light to the nations,
>   to open the eyes that are
>   blind,
> to bring out the prisoners
>   from the dungeon,
>   from the prison those who
>   sit in darkness.
>   —Isaiah 42:6-7

I would like to end this chapter with a sampling of stories written by women who have come a long way in their journey toward wholeness. The names evoke the stories of abuse described earlier. It must be said that none of the women since the earlier 1990s say they are "completely healed," though some are optimistic they are "well on their way." One, in particular, admits she has all the characteristics of emotional and spiritual codependence, has undergone psychiatric care, and took several years to sever ties with the priest who sexually abused her. Another is finding it very difficult to break off the relationship, and compares herself to an alcoholic who just cannot find the courage to quit drinking. Yet another reported the abuse to her bishop, took her case before the civil courts, and is now working very hard to regain some sense of balance in her life in spite of a court finding in her favor that awarded her a large financial settlement. Others have at least taken the first and most important step . . . they told their stories. A major stumbling block seems to be denial, not wanting to admit that the priest with whom they are in a sexual relationship is abusing his power. These women are afraid to end the relationship for fear of being lonely and of being further victimized. For them, the priest, the parish or community, the church and their Catholic faith are all parts of one same reality. Trying to break free of the hold the priest has on them so that they can heal their unhealthy condition seems to mean, in their minds, that they must let go of it all or be rejected by it all. As one woman put it, "I felt as if I'd been excommunicated because I reported an abusive priest to his bishop."

For the women like Nancy, the healing process is not quite as long or difficult, probably because they were less vulnerable to begin with. Also, they have a support system either in their family, their religious community, or a support group. While most of them chose to distance themselves from the hierarchical church for a time, they still consider themselves Christians, members of the church, Body of Christ, and people of God. But, as one member of a women-church community explains, "We see, we do, we live church *differently*."

The difference in the recovery of these two types of women seems to hinge on several factors—their degree of vulnerability, the nature of the violation, and the level of faith education that enables them to make the distinction between religious power and Christian faith. As we shall see, the outcome for Jean and Lynn speak for themselves.

JOCELYN'S RECOVERY

My return to life began the day my psychiatrist begged me to talk to someone at the sexual assault clinic. That was the most difficult step of all because I saw myself as still deeply in love with Michael, and I missed him terribly. The counselor who saw me at the clinic asked me what I loved about him and invited me to relive, moment by moment, how my relationship with him unfolded. What strikes me now, as I look back, is that she never blamed me, she didn't accuse me of being a dreamer or mentally unstable. She seemed to understand how very much I loved Michael. Very gently, however, she brought me to the place where I understood how vulnerable and needy I was when I met him and that I agreed to sleep with him to forget how lonely my life was. I gradually began to feel a great deal of anger. I trusted this man, and he used me to satisfy his sexual needs. After several sessions with the sexual assault worker, she asked me if I was interested in getting together with a few other women who met on a regular basis to discuss spiritual issues. I was not interested. I still went to Mass every Sunday but would leave in such a rage that I would become deeply depressed. I couldn't forget Michael; I really didn't think I could live without having him in my life. Then his bishop transferred him to another city.

I used to call him every day, and even went to see him. Part of me, however, wanted to break up, to just not need him anymore. I was also beginning to realize how our conversations and our time together made me more dissatisfied than anything else. In desperation, I joined the women's group.

I knew nothing about these women. They were very kind to me, as if they knew that I was hurting. In time, I became good friends with one of them who told me she had been abused by her pastor when she was younger and had given up going to Mass long ago. However, she enjoyed this group because she learned to meditate on Scripture and to pray. Over a period of several months, I went through all the stages of grief with the help of my assault clinic worker, the women at the group, and my psychiatrist. I needed to grieve the death of my marriage and my breakup with Michael.

With the support of my women's group, I wrote a letter to my bishop and his financial administrator to ask for financial assistance because I couldn't afford a psychotherapist. Probably because the letter was notarized, on my psychiatrist's advice (one of our group happened to be a lawyer), the diocese paid for my therapy and also my tuition to upgrade my nursing course and find a new job . . . on the condition that I not tell anyone and that I have nothing to do with Michael ever again. I used the money to move to another town and to find a job. My friends in the group gave me the name of a support group where I now live.

Today I still live alone, but I've reconnected with my kids. My job took me closer to where they are now living. We got some family counseling. I still felt very guilty about my marriage breaking down and the divorce. The kids were still very resentful of the way their father treated them. I notice now, though, that as I learn to put things into perspective, and learn to love myself a bit more and develop my own spirituality, my children take more control over their own lives. I hope they have some kind of reconciliation with their father who abandoned them, someday, but I'm not pushing them. I've learned to trust that they can make good decisions for themselves. They're adults now. One thing that amazes us whenever we get together now, is that we can laugh together. We can be brutally honest with one another, but we try very hard never to be unkind. There seems to be a lot less bitterness among us.

I must admit I've put some distance between myself and the Catholic Church. I'm not even sure I believe in God anymore, but I've developed an interest in Native spirituality and its healing circles. Not long ago, I met a nun who is familiar with both Christian doctrine and Native healing. I think I'd like to explore the Gospels with her. My job brings me into contact with Native women in prison. I have been journeying with one of them because she wants to bring a civil suit against a missionary priest who raped and beat her when she was a little girl in a residential school . . .

NANCY'S RECOVERY

When I lost my job as pastoral assistant in my parish, I became very depressed. My family doctor suggested I consult a psychotherapist. She in turn advised me to join an Al-Anon Group because she believed, from what I told her, that my husband was an alcoholic, and I had all the classic signs of being codependent. She also said that, with regard to my job, I was behaving like a battered woman because I was afraid to confront the priest who had fired me. I was very skeptical about all of this. I felt that if I prayed more everything would turn out all right. Instead, I became more and more isolated and spent my days watching TV or sleeping.

One evening my husband was arrested for drunk driving. I was in the car with him and was so terrified (he was driving much too fast) that I had to admit that he really did have a drinking problem. I decided to attend Al-Anon meetings to find out how to help him solve his problem. I went to the meetings for several months, but was too afraid to tell my husband. I was too scared that he would get angry at me and leave me. At those Al-Anon meetings I discovered that I really was codependent. I wanted to solve my husband's problem, but in fact, my problem was that I had lost all control over my own life. My job at the parish made me feel validated as a Christian woman, but, deep down, all my life I had been trying to find God's love through the approval of the clergy.

I came to understand that I had to change, and that it wasn't up to me to change my husband. So, the first thing I did was give myself permission to rest when I felt tired. I worked the Twelve Steps, and started to meditate to find my center, my self-esteem, and my lost boundaries. I went on a retreat, and in the course of one of my meditations remembered I had been sexually abused by my grandfather as a child. Perhaps that is what explained the difficulty I had expressing affection, especially with my husband. One day, I managed to find the courage to ask him to go for marriage counseling with me. He agreed to try it and, in the course of our counseling, admitted that he drank because he was trying to drown his fear of losing me. I was so "dedicated" to the church that there was no more room for him in my life. He even thought I was having an affair with one of the priests at the parish. We cleared away a lot of garbage in those counseling sessions, and discovered that our marriage and our family were very important to both of us.

I eventually left the Al-Anon group because I was looking for something more specifically Christian and Gospel-based. Jack and I had started going back to Mass, but we didn't feel particularly welcome or nurtured spiritually. One day, Jack ran into a priest who had been involved with him in a youth group many years ago and who was looking to start a base community. He asked Jack if he might be interested. We agreed, reluctantly. Jack was a very devout Catholic as a youngster but had become very suspicious of clergy, especially as one pedophilia scandal broke after another. I was afraid of "getting sucked in" once again. But the base community didn't work "hierarchically." All decisions were made by consensus. Every woman and man in the group was called upon to exercise their gifts and talents. The main purpose was to live according to the Word of God, to learn to pray together, and help the needy.

We were going through a particularly hard time with our kids. Our daughter had had an abortion, one of our sons went to jail for drug trafficking. I had started to do volunteer work at a hospital and the chaplaincy people saw talents in me for pastoral work among terminally ill patients. With a bit more training, I could be hired full time at that kind of a job. My husband supported me 100 percent and offered to pay for my university courses. These days, he's thinking of retiring from his business, but not me. I spent four years getting my life back together and I love my work. And even though Jack is much more comfortable working in his garden and fixing antique cars than discussing theology, he listens to me and has lots of very sound practical advice for me in dealing with the folks he calls my "clients." . . .

Sister Jean, whose story is included briefly in chapter 5, shared the following with me at a women's conference we both attended about a year prior to this writing. It had been almost ten years since she first told me about losing her position as a project director in her former diocese.

When I realized my position would not be waiting for me when I came back from my sick leave, I considered leaving my community. I felt totally useless. One of our sisters who lived in a neighboring diocese asked me to come and lead a retreat being offered to lay pastoral assistants. At the end of the weekend, one woman asked if I would come and speak to her Bible study group made up of about five married couples. I could sense their deep spiritual thirst and profound prayer life. That was the beginning of a whole new ministry for me, which my new bishop supported. Today I head up a team that helps small groups of adults with their faith development and prayer life. I was sent away for further training, obtained a graduate degree in theology and spirituality and now train facilitators for groups who want to either form a small base community or lay communities of married couples affiliated to religious communities. Our focus is on openness to and discernment of the gifts of the Spirit. After several years of this ministry, I was called upon to serve in the leadership team of my community. Had I not been surrounded by the support and affirmation of my sisters in community and close friends, I can't imagine how I would have begun to heal the wounds of abuse of power that I—and many others like me—have suffered at the hands of ambitious clergymen.

It is the sequel to Lynn's story that finally persuaded me of the importance of recording all these stories of abuse of power. Lynn, who finally divorced the violent man she had married against the advice of her pastor, left the church. She considers herself a spiritual person but will have nothing to do with organized religion. She told me, although she hoped I would include her story in my book, that she was seriously skeptical that anything would be done at the institutional level to change things. She sees the Catholic Church as hopelessly misogynist and dysfunctional. She has withdrawn her children from Catholic schools and organizes family activities on Sundays other than attending church. Lynn recognizes that she still harbors a great deal of anger and inability to forgive herself for following her pastor's advice and not leaving the marriage sooner. Her children also bear the scars of emotional and physical abuse, and have needed psychiatric care. Lynn worked at two jobs for years to put herself through college and eventually became a clinical psychologist. This has enabled her to support her family and provide them with the care they need. But in our last conversation, she is still searching for healing of her spirit and recovery of the soul she was robbed of as a child.

Readings

Many women are uncomfortable reading the Bible or using it as inspiration for prayer because of its patriarchal language and largely male imagery for the divine. If that is the case, I strongly recommend that support group leaders read and refer to Sandra M. Schneiders, *The Bible and Feminism: Biblical Theology* in Catherine Mowry LaCugna, ed., *Freeing Theology, The Essentials of Theology in Feminist Perspective.* An interesting alternative is Miriam Therese Winter, *The Gospel According to Mary: A New Testament for Women* (New York: Crossroad, 1994).

Among a host of books for prayer and meditation, I heartily recommend *The Psalms, Meditations for Every Day of the Year* by Joan Chittister (New York: Crossroad, 1996); and *Exploring the Feminine Face of God* by Bridget Mary Meehan, s.s.c. (Kansas City, MO: Sheed & Ward, 1991).

Notes

1. Bible excerpts are taken from The New Revised Standard Version, Catholic Edition, 1993 (see copyright page).

2. Yvonne Maes, *The Cannibal's Wife: A Memoir* (New York: Herodias, 1999) 251–252.

CONCLUSION

A disturbing story that appeared in the international press in March 2001 reported that in more than twenty countries, Catholic priests had used their spiritual authority to gain sexual favors from women religious and secondary school students. In June of that same year, Sr. Myra Poole, the coordinator of an international conference on the ordination of women in Dublin, Ireland, and Sr. Joan Chittister, a keynote speaker, both attended the conference in spite of strong-arm tactics of the Vatican to discourage them. These two seemingly unrelated reports are but two examples of the oppression of women that still plagues the Catholic Church. Sadly, these very public reports corroborate the personal and private stories of countless Catholic women around the globe.

The stories that have been recounted here are intended to illustrate that when spiritual power is used to manipulate, control, debilitate, or discredit, it can make its victims physically, emotionally, and spiritually ill. Indeed, how often have we not heard the comment, "Those people are sick!" when complaints of sexual misconduct are brought forward by women in the church. There are those who would prefer to see these victims as unstable, hypersensitive, frail, or obsessed with the idea of either seducing a priest or having access to power themselves. It is true that many Catholic women who have suffered an abuse of power by a clergy member are very unwell. What this book has tried to document is that their problems are caused by the systemic inequality between men and women still operating in the church's doctrine, laws, and liturgy. It was in the hope of helping to bind the wounds inflicted by men entrusted with the sacred power of the priesthood that I recorded the stories women shared with me. I searched for common symptoms, a plausible cause and a spiritual path to prescribe and follow to find healing.

The codependence and addiction model is particularly suitable to describe women who are in a sexual relationship with a priest or who experience sexual harassment and exploitation at the hands of the priests and bishops for whom they work. That is because the addiction to power at work within the clergy affects the laity, which includes all women, by keeping them in a state of dependence for access to the sacred in their lives. It will come as no surprise, therefore, that to recover from the effect of abuse of spiritual power, women establish a relationship with the divine elsewhere than in the institutional church, its rites, sacraments, and patriarchal priestly ministry.

The object of this book, and this bears repeating, is to help women recover from the harmful effects of abuse of power. Some may find it contains some rather caustic comments about the clergy and the church as an institution, but that was not my intent. As baptized persons, disciples of Jesus, we have a duty to speak the truth to power, even about as painful a problem as clergy sexual misconduct and exploitation of the laity. Not to do so, not to recognize that relationships between women and clergy are unhealthy precisely because women and men are not equal in the Catholic Church, is to refuse to recognize the truth. Not to seek the truth about a church problem because those who are in power do not authorize us to do so would, in fact, be dysfunctional.

The issue of Rome's refusal to ordain women is another element of this truth-seeking. That is because admission to holy orders gives a voice in decision-making and policy-setting within the church as a human institution. It would also allow women to minister sacramentally to other women. Still, church authorities claim they have the right to exclude women because the church is a divine, all-male hierarchical institution founded by Jesus Christ himself. It stands by this claim in spite of the overwhelming scholarly evidence that Jesus of Nazareth did no such thing. By refusing to admit women to holy orders, the current church leadership has become entrenched in its unwillingness to allow women to express to the whole church their perception of themselves as persons, their experience of God and their understanding of the mission Christ entrusted to his disciples. To stifle the voice of the Holy Spirit that speaks to the whole church through women is an institutional sin of sexism that touches the lives of all Catholics.

A process of conversion needs to be undertaken to acknowledge the work of the Spirit in the lives of women. Scripture teaches us that women too were called to become disciples of Jesus, and that in Christ, there is to be no inequality because of race, social status, or gender. The conversion needed within the church, for all its members, is a turning away from what Bishop Alexander Carter called in the wake of the Second Vatican Council, "the original sin of patriarchy."[1] This does not mean that we must do away with structure, or even the episcopal model of church. It does mean that all members of the church are part of a holy priesthood, and that members called to ordained ministries within the structure must be open to current theological and scriptural research, and progress in the human sciences, as well as to the fact that the Spirit's gifts of authority, teaching, healing, and governing are not given only to some unmarried men.

Until that happens, women in the church will continue to experience fear and frustration. Still, we must continue to take the risk of speaking out for justice. Conversion for us is to open our hearts to the Spirit of wisdom and find in her the strength to say to those in authority who cling to their power: this is wrong, this has to change, this is hurting the people of God. We will be ridiculed, dismissed, and even punished—as Jesus was for speaking the truth to power. We have a duty to insist that our truth be heard so that those who are in a position to change things will let themselves be moved to do the just and right thing. Speaking the truth to power can be a catalyst for true conversion and evangelization.

Conversion begins for both women and clergy with justice-making. Where there has been an injustice committed, there must be reconciliation. This requires recognition of and repentance for wrongdoing. Repentance, the expression of regret, the willingness to make amends, and the resolve to change are the elements of reconciliation. Making amends should take the form of a concrete gesture that indicates to the offended person that the offender has the intent and the desire to make things right. But if the clergy persists in denying any kind of wrongdoing, in refusing to take responsibility for injustices perpetrated against women; if it turns a deaf ear to reports of morally reprehensible acts, reconciliation will never happen. None of the women I interviewed during my research experienced true reconciliation with the priest who abused his power.

This is not to say that the official church has not recognized that there is a problem, or that individual dioceses do not have policies in place to deal with this issue. It does mean that those policies often do not translate into action in favor of true reconciliation and healing. The focus still seems to be on protecting the priest's reputation and the integrity of the institution at the expense of the victims. There have sometimes been official apologies made on behalf of individual dioceses, but while they express regret at what has happened, they fall short of admitting that what the individual cleric did was unacceptable. Either the offending priests believe they are above asking for forgiveness or they are consistently advised not to do so for fear of legal prosecution. And yet, so many of the victims who ended up before the civil courts would not have gone that route if there had been a real attempt at reconciliation.

Many women who were subjected to abuse of power in their church work finally admitted to themselves that the sexism they experienced is part of a larger problem and inconsistent with the Gospel. Others still do not acknowledge that it is the system itself that is conducive to codependence. They prefer to believe that they can change the system by continuing to work within it, in the hope of some day having a voice in decisions being made about them and for them. They do not feel they are being treated unfairly when they are denied the fullness of sacramental life by not being admitted into holy orders. Some realize this is discriminatory but remain in the church because they believe the hierarchy and clergy are not the whole church. Others simply leave. They have given up any hope of ever changing the system or even adjusting to it, since the hierarchical and patriarchal nature of the contemporary Catholic Church is, in their view, fundamentally male-centered and irretrievably misogynous.

It is painful for these women to leave the church. They are strongly tempted to stay on because the community and the rituals have been familiar and reassuring for so long. Those who leave the church speak of experiencing a time of intense loneliness. Nevertheless, to recover their personal worth and dignity, to find new ways of understanding and naming the divine reality, and to follow Christ more faithfully, they accepted to go into exile. They deprive themselves of liturgical celebrations, especially the Eucharist, and give up their work in a church setting if it means being continually kept silent and invisible. Many of them are aware of the addiction to power within church structures and their own codependence regarding it. Resolved to become more fully alive, interdependent with others but not dependent on clergy approval to live out their faith commitment, they seek out or simply create other faith communities.

Among those who distance themselves from the institutional Catholic Church, but refuse to leave, claiming it is possible to be both Catholic and feminist, there are those who gravitate toward smaller faith communities on the margins of mainstream parishes. These women firmly believe that they too "are the church," members of the Body of Christ, the people of God. They feel a sense of alienation, of being in exile in their own church because they are not fully recognized as persons within it. They deplore that by not recognizing, as does Scripture (Gal 3:28) the equal dignity of women and men in Christ, the hierarchy is not following its own teaching:

> True, all persons are not alike from the point of view of varying physical power and the diversity of intellectual and moral

resources. Nevertheless, with respect to the fundamental rights of the person, every type of discrimination, whether social or cultural, whether based on sex, race, color, social condition, language or religion is to be overcome and eradicated as contrary to God's intent (*Gaudium et Spes*, no. 29).

While admitting women to holy orders would give them visibility and a voice, it will not of itself end discrimination and abuse of power. It is the current model of priesthood, based on the dualistic paradigm of clergy versus laity, sacred versus profane, which is in need of reform, and not only because it is inherently and essentially sexist. By restricting the power to celebrate the sacraments, in particular the Eucharist, to unmarried men, the hierarchy of the Catholic Church is jeopardizing the future of the church as a sacramental community. For if we are to believe that the Eucharist is the "crown and summit" of the Liturgy (Pius XII), or as the Second Vatican Council put it, "the fount and apex" of the church, then Eucharist must be held up as the center of the church's activity, the source of her strength, her very life. We must therefore, as faithful Catholics, continue to press the Vatican to change its regulations about an exclusively unmarried male clergy. The people of God have a right to the Eucharist, a right that supersedes the restrictions of gender or marital status on the ministerial priesthood. We are losing the Eucharist for lack of priests. That is far more damaging to the Catholic Church and of far greater consequence than changing canon law to admit women and married men to holy orders.

The more we lose even weekly Eucharist in so many places, remote and not so remote, the more the very life of the people of God is weakened. Communion services—presided by lay men and women—are not the solution. They are detrimental in that they separate the liturgical action from its completion: they separate the symbolic breaking of the bread and sharing of the saving cup from the action of coming together and being commissioned to live a Christ-like life. There was a time when Sunday Eucharist was required of every Catholic under pain of mortal sin—an absolute requirement. Now it is subject to the availability of unmarried males. Stopgap measures such as Communion services are teaching the faithful the theologically abhorrent fiction that Eucharist is not essential to being church.

Actually, the whole idea of priesthood instituted for celebrating the eucharistic sacrifice at Mass needs to be revisited. In keeping with new theologies, notably liberation theology and feminist theologies, the Church of Rome needs to move away from an image of God whose anger needs to be appeased. Jesus died because he called political and religious systems to change. God did not exact the human sacrifice: men did. Already the prophets of the Old Testament were on to that insight: God does not take pleasure in the pain of humans or animals; God wants justice and compassion for humanity and all creation. Twice Matthew's Gospel has Jesus say: "Go and learn what this means: I desire mercy, not sacrifice" (Matt 9:13 and 12:7). It was true two thousand years ago, and is still true now that it is often Jerusalem (the symbol of religious authority) that kills the prophets. Jesus was no exception. And when Jesus asks us to pick up our cross and follow him, he is not advocating self-immolation, but he is rather calling us to confront violence with proactive and creative love. As church, are we not also called to reject a sacrificial form of worship conducive to all kinds of abuse of power and embrace one another as a holy people whose Eucharist—thanksgiving—celebrates God's reign which is truth, justice, and compassion for all who suffer?

Notes

1. Alex Carter, *A Canadian Bishop's Memoir*, 223.

Appendix 1

ARE YOU IN AN ABUSIVE RELATIONSHIP WITH A PRIEST?

1. What first made you aware there might be a problem in your relationship with this priest?

2. Is your relationship with this priest secret and exclusive, does it involve any kind of sexual activity (deep kissing, fondling, masturbation, sexual intercourse)?

3. Do you feel guilty about this relationship, wondering if it is appropriate?

4. Do you feel that you are investing more into this relationship than you are getting from it?

5. Even if you are not sexually involved, do you often meet alone? Are you inclined to be jealous of other women in the priest's life?

6. Does the priest act inappropriately with you (personal gifts such as lingerie, off-color jokes, comments on your appearance, questions about your sex life)?

7. If you are in an intimate relationship with the priest, has he used his priesthood as a pretext not to marry you?

8. Does he talk more about his needs and his problems, neglecting your concerns in the course of a pastoral relationship? Does he brag about women who have "fallen for him"?

9. Does the priest discourage you from getting on with your life, becoming more independent, seeking spiritual direction, or emotional help elsewhere?

10. Have your family or close friends ever expressed distrust of his motives?

11. Has his bishop or another priest told him to stay away from you or vice-versa?

12. Have you sacrificed a great deal of time, energy or money to keep him in your life?

13. Do you feel you have to lie about this relationship because others won't understand?

14. Do you find it difficult to pray or attend Mass if this priest is not presiding?

15. Do you always give in to his needs, desires, requests at the expense of your own?

If you suspect you have been abused by a priest, call the chancery office of your diocese and ask for a copy of the diocesan policy for dealing with allegations of clergy misconduct.

Appendix 2

ARE YOU BEING EXPLOITED
BY THE CHURCH?

1. Have you recently been dismissed from your church employment with no explanation?

2. Did you have a contract with the parish or the diocese? Were you given the opportunity to discuss the job description, such as tasks, hours, salary, and work conditions?

3. Do you often accept to do work that is not in your job description?

4. Do you feel guilty if you have to refuse? Do you get paid for working overtime?

5. Do you take great care not to express an opinion that would displease your employer?

6. Are you made to feel responsible every time something goes wrong in your workplace or when your employer makes a mistake?

7. Do you have a tendency to overlook obvious injustices in your workplace?

8. Has the priest in your workplace ever sexually harassed you, e.g., kissing you on the mouth instead of the cheek, hugging you too close, talking about his sexual problems, telling dirty jokes, standing too close, "accidentally" touching your breasts?

9. Do you often get calls at home outside of working hours or on your day off?

10. Do you easily "forgive and forget" when you are unfairly punished or reprimanded or publicly humiliated?

11. Have you developed the habit of not making any decisions about your activities with your family and friends that your employer might not approve for fear of being fired?

12. Do you find yourself eating, drinking, working excessively, or taking medication to relieve the stress at work?

13. Do you consistently give up time with your family or sacrifice a great deal of time, energy and money for "the good of the church"?

14. Have you sacrificed some of your principles to keep your job (lying, cheating, sexual favors)?

15. Do you tend to overlook the fact that your spouse, community, children have suffered because you dedicate too much time to your work?

BIBLIOGRAPHY

ARCHDIOCESAN COMMISSION OF ENQUIRY, The Report of the Archdiocesan Commission of Enquiry into the Sexual Abuse of Children by Members of the Clergy, Conclusions and Recommendations. St. John's Newfoundland: Diocese of St. John's, 1990.

ASSEMBLY OF QUEBEC BISHOPS, A Heritage of Violence? Montreal, 1989.

Canadian Conference of Catholic Bishops, From Pain to Hope. Ottawa: Concacan, Inc., 1992.

Carlson Brown, Johanne, and Carole R. Bohn, eds. Christianity, Patriarchy and Abuse: A Feminist Critique. New York: Pilgrim Press, 1989.

Carr, Anne E. Transforming Grace. New York: Continuum, 1996.

Carter, Alex. A Canadian Bishop's Memoir. North Bay: Tomiko Publications, 1994.

Catechism of the Catholic Church. New York: Doubleday, 1994.

Chittister, Joan. The Psalms, Meditations for Every Day of the Year. New York: Crossroad, 1996.

Crosby, Michael H. The Dysfunctional Church, Addiction and Codependency in the Family of Catholicism. Notre Dame, IN: Ave Maria Press, 1991.

Cummings, Louise. Eyes Wide Open: Spiritual Resources for Healing from Childhood Sexual Assault. Winfield, WV: Woodland Books, 1994.

Fortune, Marie Marshall. Sexual Violence, The Unmentionable Sin. New York: Pilgrim Press, 1983.

———. Is Nothing Sacred? Cleveland: United Church Press, 1999.

Fortune, Marie Marshall, and James N. Poling. *Sexual Abuse by Clergy: A Crisis for the Church*. Decatur, GA: Journal of Pastoral Care Publications, Inc., 1994.

Fortune, Marie Marshall, and others. *Clergy Misconduct: An Educational Curriculum for Clergy and Religious Professionals*. Seattle, WA: Centre for the Prevention of Sexual and Domestic Violence, 1992.

Frankel, Lois P. *Women, Anger and Depression: Strategies for Self-Empowerment*. Los Angeles: Health Communications, Inc., 1992.

Griffiths, Josephine, *Seeking Sophia: Meditations and Reflections for Women Who No Longer Go to Church*. Toronto: Novalis, 1997.

Harris, Maria. *Dance of the Spirit: The Seven Steps of Women's Spirituality*. New York: Bantam Books, 1991.

Hoffman, Virginia Curran. *The Codependent Church*. New York: Crossroad, 1991.

Jay, Nancy. "Sacrifice and Social Structure in Christianity." In *Throughout Your Generations Forever*. Chicago: University of Chicago Press, 1992.

John Paul II. *Letter to Women*, 1995 (www.vatican.va).

———. *Mulieris Dignitatem*. On the Dignity and Vocation of Women, September 30, 1988 (www.vatican.va).

———. *Ordination Sacerdotalis*. Apostolic Letter on Ordination and Women, in *Origins*, Vol. 24, No. 4, 1994.

Johnson, Elizabeth A., *She Who Is: The Mystery of God in Feminist Theological Discourse*. New York: Crossroad, 1993.

———. *Consider Jesus: Waves of Renewal in Christology*. New York: Crossroad, 1999.

———. *Friends of God and Prophets: A Feminist Theological Reading of the Communion of Saints*. New York: Continuum, 1998.

Kennedy, Eugene. *The Unhealed Wound, The Church and Human Sexuality*. New York: St. Martin's Press, 2001.

LaCugna, Catherine Mowry, ed., Freeing Theology: The Essentials of Theology in Feminist Perspective. San Francisco: Harper Collins, 1993.

Maes, Yvonne. The Cannibal's Wife: A Memoir. New York: Herodias, 1999.

Manning, Joanna. Is the Pope Catholic? A Woman Confronts Her Church. Toronto: Malcom Lester Books, 1999.

———. Take Back the Truth. Crossroad: New York, 2002.

McEwan, Dorothea, ed. Women Experiencing Church: A Documentation of Alienation. Montreal: Novalis, 1991.

Meehan, Bridget Mary, s.s.c. Exploring the Feminine Face of God. Kansas City, MO: Sheed & Ward, 1991.

Mellody, Pia. Facing Codependency. San Francisco: Harper Collins, 1989.

Moltmann, Jürgen, and Elisabeth Moltmann-Wendell. Passion for God: Theology in Two Voices. Louisville, KY: Westminster John Knox Press, 2003.

National Conference of Bishops (U.S.). "'Called to Be One in Christ Jesus.' Pastoral on Concerns of Women." Origins Vol. 21, No. 46, April 23, 1992.

Osiek, Carolyn. Beyond Anger: On Being a Feminist in the Church. New York: Paulist Press, 1986.

Papesh, Michael L. Clerical Culture: Contradiction and Transformation. Collegeville, MN: Liturgical Press, 2004.

Pellauer, Mary E., Barbara Chester, and Jane Boyajian, eds. Sexual Assault and Abuse, A Handbook for Clergy and Religious Professionals. San Francisco: Harper and Row, 1987.

Radford Ruether, Rosemary. Sexism and God-Talk. Boston: Beacon Press, 1983.

———. "Women's Difference and Equal Rights in the Church." In The Power of Naming: A Concilium Reader in Feminist Liberation Theology. E. Schüssler Fiorenza, ed. New York: Orbis Books, 1996.

Runcorn, David. *A Centre of Quiet: Hearing God When Life Is Noisy.* Downers Grove, IL: InterVarsity Press, 1990.

Rutter, Peter. *Sex in the Forbidden Zone.* New York: St. Martin's Press, 1989.

Sands, Kathleen. "Secret Heartaches: Priestly Celibacy and the Women It Touches." In *Escape from Paradise.* Minneapolis: Fortress Press, 1994.

Schaef, Anne Wilson. *Codependence: Misunderstood—Mistreated.* Harper-SanFranciso, 1986.

————. *When Society Becomes an Addict.* San Francisco: Harper and Row, 1987.

————. *Women's Reality: An Emerging Female System in a White Male Society.* Minneapolis: Winston, 1985.

Schneiders, Sandra M. *Beyond Patching, Faith and Feminism in the Catholic Church.* Mahwah, NJ: Paulist Press, 1991.

Schüssler Fiorenza, Elisabeth. *In Memory of Her: A Feminist Theological Reconstruction of Christian Origins.* New York: Crossroad, 1983.

————. *But SHE Said. Feminist Practices of Biblical Interpretations.* Boston: Beacon Press, 1992.

Shupe, Anson, ed. *Wolves Within the Fold: Religious Leadership and Abuse of Power.* New Brunswick, NJ: Rutgers University Press, 1998.

Ward, Hannah, Jennifer Wild, and Janet Morley. *Celebrating Women (The New Edition).* Harrisburg, PA: Morehouse Publishing, 1995.

Washburn, Penelope. *Becoming Woman: The Quest for Wholeness in Female Experience.* New York: Harper and Row, 1977.

Winter, Miriam Therese. *The Gospel According to Mary: A New Testament for Women.* New York: Crossroad, 1994.

INDEX